*Algernon Charles*
Swinburne

Shearsman Classics Vol. 28

**Titles in the *Shearsman Classics* series:**

1. *Poets of Devon and Cornwall, from Barclay to Coleridge*
2. Robert Herrick: *Selected Poems*
3. *Spanish Poetry of the Golden Age in contemporary English translations*
4. Mary, Lady Chudleigh: *Selected Poems*
5. William Strode: *Selected Poems*
6. Sir Thomas Wyatt: *Selected Poems*
7. *Tottel's Miscellany* (1557) *(The Tudor Miscellanies, Vol. 1)*
8. *The Phoenix Nest* (1593) *(The Tudor Miscellanies, Vol. 2)*
9. *England's Helicon* (1600) *(The Tudor Miscellanies, Vol. 3)*
10. Mary Coleridge: *Selected Poems*
11. D.H. Lawrence: *Look! We Have Come Through!*
12. D.H. Lawrence: *Birds, Beasts and Flowers*
13. D.H. Lawrence: *Studies in Classic American Literature*
14. Johann Wolfgang von Goethe: *Faust* (translated by Mike Smith)
15. Robert Browning: *Dramatic Romances*
16. Robert Browning: *Sordello*
17. Robert Browning: *The Ring and the Book*
18. Fernando de Herrera: *Selected Poems*
    (translated by Michael Smith & Luis Ingelmo)
19. Thomas Gray: *The English Poems*
20. John Donne: *Poems (1633)*
21. Antonio Machado: *Solitudes and Other Early Poems*
    (translated by Michael Smith & Luis Ingelmo)
22. Thomas Carew: *Collected Poems*
23. Gérard de Nerval: *Les Chimères* (translated by Will Stone)
24. Gerard Manley Hopkins: *The Wreck of the Deutschland* (ed. by Nigel Foxell)
25. Sir John Suckling: *Collected Poems*
26. Richard Lovelace: *Collected Poems*
27. Robert Herrick: *Hesperides* (1648)
28. A.C. Swinburne: *Our Lady of Pain*

# Our Lady of Pain

*Poems of Eros and Perversion*

# Algernon Charles Swinburne

Edited and introduced by
Mark Scroggins

Shearsman Books

Published in the United Kingdom in 2019 by
Shearsman Books Ltd

www.shearsman.com

ISBN 978-1-84861-645-5

Notes and editorial matter
copyright © Mark Scroggins 2019

# Contents

| | |
|---|---|
| Introduction | 7 |
| Further Reading | 12 |
| A Note on the Texts | 12 |
| | |
| from *Chastelard: A Tragedy* | 15 |
| | |
| A Ballad of Life | 17 |
| Laus Veneris | 20 |
| Les Noyades | 34 |
| Anactoria | 37 |
| Hermaphroditus | 45 |
| Fragoletta | 47 |
| Satia Te Sanguine | 50 |
| In the Orchard | 53 |
| A Match | 55 |
| Faustine | 57 |
| A Cameo | 63 |
| The Leper | 64 |
| Erotion | 69 |
| Before Dawn | 71 |
| Dolores | 74 |
| Sapphics | 87 |
| | |
| from The Masque of Queen Bersabe | 90 |
| | |
| Love and Sleep | 97 |
| Cleopatra | 98 |
| | |
| from Pasiphae [a dramatic fragment] | 102 |
| | |
| The Complaint of the Fair Armouress | 108 |
| | |
| from *Tristram of Lyonesse* | 111 |
| | |
| Explanatory Notes | 118 |

# Introduction

The scion of two aristocratic families, Algernon Charles Swinburne was born in 1837 in London and spent his childhood on the Isle of Wight and at his grandfather's estate in Northumberland. He attended Eton and then Balliol College, Oxford, where he met and became fast friends with the Pre-Raphaelites Dante Gabriel Rossetti, William Morris, and Edward Burne-Jones. He had already published two verse plays when *Atalanta in Calydon* was released in 1865 to considerable acclaim. The following year, *Poems and Ballads* generated a firestorm of critical and public controversy: without gainsaying their extraordinary formal and musical accomplishments, reviewers attacked Swinburne's poems for their licentiousness and anti-theism. His publisher withdrew the book within days of publication, and he was forced to transfer his works to another house.

Swinburne had invoked the doctrine of 'art for art's sake' (derived from Théophile Gautier and Charles Baudelaire) in defence of *Poems and Ballads*, but his next collection *Songs Before Sunrise* (1870) was a profoundly politically committed book, its poems dealing with the Italian *Risorgimento* and the more general human striving for freedom. That collection, the plays *Bothwell* (1874) and *Erectheus* (1876), and the 1878 *Poems and Ballads, Second Series* were far more favourably received by critics and the general reading public than the first *Poems and Ballads* had been.

Through the 1870s Swinburne was prodigiously active, publishing collections of poetry, plays, and critical studies. But his personal life was in alarming disarray, and his alcoholic dissipation forecast an almost certain early grave. In 1879, he was 'rescued' by the lawyer and writer Theodore Watts (later Watts-Dunton), who took him to a suburban retreat in Putney, weaned him from his drinking habit, and became his companion and *de facto* guardian for the rest of his life.

In Putney, Swinburne enjoyed a remarkably serene and sheltered existence and continued to produce poetry, dramas, and criticism. Although the scandal of the 1866 *Poems and Ballads* was never quite forgotten by readers of Swinburne's later, far less transgressive verse, moral opprobrium was largely displaced by respect for his lyrical and metrical talents. By the last decade of the century Swinburne was widely regarded, with Tennyson and Browning, as one of the three greatest poets of his time. On the laureate Tennyson's death in 1892, Queen Victoria is said to have observed, 'I am told that Mr Swinburne is the best poet in my dominions'. (He was not offered the laureateship.) When Swinburne died peacefully of pneumonia in 1909, W. B. Yeats pronounced, 'Now I am king of the cats'.

No Victorian poet suffered a more precipitous decline in reputation in the twentieth century than Swinburne. T. S. Eliot's criticisms (in 'Swinburne as Poet', 1920)—that Swinburne's work is 'diffuse', 'imprecise', metrically over-facile, and ultimately untethered to concrete reality—became common currency of dismissals of the poet. There is some truth to these critiques, and Swinburne certainly wrote far too much on trivial subjects in his later years. His formal and musical mastery, however, cannot be denied, and more recent readers have found in his work a surprising precision of language and subtlety and complexity of thought.

\* \* \*

The present selection of Swinburne's verse focuses precisely on what the first reviewers of the 1866 *Poems and Ballads* found most objectionable: erotic passion, in both its 'normal' and 'perverse' varieties. The anonymous review for the *London Review* called the poems 'depraved and morbid in the last degree'; Robert Buchanan in the *Athenaeum* pronounced Swinburne 'unclean for the sake of uncleanness'; and John Morley, in the most thorough and eloquent of the attacks (in the *Saturday Review*), called the poems 'nameless shameless abominations', Swinburne's 'a mind all aflame with the feverish carnality of a schoolboy over the dirtiest passages in Lemprière', and Swinburne himself 'the libidinous laureate of a pack of satyrs'.

Contemporary readers are less likely to condemn a poet for hinting at or even outrightly depicting sex, but Swinburne's treatment of physical passion, and the varieties of passion about which he chose to write, retain the power to shock. Certainly there are a variety of non-normative sexual situations to be found in his poems: same-sex desire in 'Anactoria' and other 'sapphic' poems; necrophilia in 'The Leper'; transsexualism in 'Hermaphroditus' and 'Fragoletta'; bestiality in the fragment 'Pasiphae'. Most evident in the *Poems and Ballads* selections is Swinburne's algolagnia, in which sexual 'pleasure' is closely associated with physical or spiritual 'pain'.

Swinburne's own sexual life remains somewhat mysterious. One suspects that the hearty homoerotic banter and the schoolboy enthusiasm for de Sade that runs through much of his correspondence are a bluff masking a paucity of actual experience. Oscar Wilde called Swinburne 'a braggart in matters of vice, who had done everything he could to convince his fellow citizens of his homosexuality and bestiality without being in the slightest degree a homosexual or bestializer'.

It appears that Swinburne had one great romantic passion—for his cousin Mary Gordon, biographers now agree—but after she married another man (the parting commemorated in 'The Triumph of Time') he never formed another. For a while he enjoyed the company of the American actress and poet Adah Isaacs Menken; apparently Swinburne's friends, dismayed that the poet remained a virgin at thirty, had arranged the liaison. To no avail: Menken could not bring him 'up to scratch'; 'I can't make him understand that biting's no use!', Edmund Gosse reported her as saying.

The one sexual—or quasi-sexual—activity in which we can be certain Swinburne participated is passive flagellation. It appears that Swinburne conceived a taste for the birch while at Eton, and continued to take pleasure in real or imagined flagellation for the rest of his life. In the 1860s, according to Gosse, he patronized 'a mysterious house in St. John's Wood where two golden-haired and rouge-cheeked ladies received, in luxuriously furnished rooms, gentlemen whom they consented to chastise for large sums'. Being whipped was at the centre of Swinburne's sexual imagination, and through most of his life he recorded explicit masochistic fantasies—in his novels, in his correspondence, and in a quantity of flagellant poems, some of them published anonymously while he was alive, but aside from metrical fluency and occasional wit not to be distinguished from the rest of the vast outpouring of Victorian flagellant pornography.[1]

Swinburne's taste for punishment as a fundamental element in the sexual relationship is epitomized in the *femmes fatales* who dominate 'Laus Veneris', 'Dolores', and 'Faustine', but the poet's masochism suffuses his works, so that even in 'The Triumph of Time', a grand and melancholy poem of leave-taking not included here, the speaker figures his greatest

---

[1] Those with a taste for punishment can consult Mark McDougal's transcription of Swinburne's largest gathering of flagellant verse, *The Flogging-Block: An Heroic Poem in A Prologue and Twelve Eclogues* (Birchgrove Press, 2011). After serious consideration, I have elected not to include any of these poems in this selection; they are of historical, biographical, and psychological—but not literary—interest.

intimacy with his beloved as one of painful submission: 'O sweet, | had you felt, lying under the palms of your feet, | The heart of my heart, beating harder with pleasure | To feel you tread it to dust and death'. Throughout his works, the word 'pleasure' is rarely encountered without 'pain' in its near neighbourhood.

There is surely an element of *épater la bourgeoisie* in Swinburne's assembling so many perversely erotic poems in *Poems and Ballads*, but this was part and parcel of his most basic impulse, that of rebellion against established conventions and powers. He is fundamentally a poet of liberty, setting himself in a line of such great rebels as Milton, Blake, Shelley, and Victor Hugo. It is a paradoxical identity, to be sure, as a number of critics have noted: for Swinburne's passionate love of freedom, his desire to be unconstrained by any social mores, religious dogmas, or other 'mind-forg'd manacles', coexists with a deep desire to abase himself before a hero-figure, whether it be a literary idol like Walter Savage Landor or Hugo, or a political leader like Giuseppe Mazzini.

This paradox is played out in his erotic poetry. Swinburne, and the speakers of his poems, crave the freedom to speak their desires and passions in ways not allowed by the constricted vocabulary of the Victorian moment. But those desires and passions themselves are, more often than not, experiences of domination, torment, and excruciating pain. Swinburne, in the prose pamphlet *Notes on Poems and Reviews*, writes of the abasement of 'Dolores' as a stage that must be passed through to reach the calm *apatheia* of 'The Garden of Proserpine' and 'Hesperia'; but his discussion glosses over the zest with which his poem recounts and revels in the cruelty of 'Our Lady of Pain'. Pain is not merely a stage through which one must pass to reach freedom; pain is itself pleasure.

If Swinburne is probably the *kinkiest* poet of the Victorian era, it's worth emphasizing that he is a master of the erotic in all its forms, to be ranked with the greatest English poets of physical love—Marlowe, Herrick, Cleveland, or Keats. His first readers were appalled by the varieties of 'perversion' on display in *Poems and Ballads*, but Victorian audiences were almost equally appalled by the forthrightness and intensity of his depiction of (non-masochistic) heterosexual passion in such poems as 'Before Dawn' and 'Love and Sleep'. The passages here included from his long Arthurian narrative *Tristram of Lyonesse*, along with the earlier selections, go far towards establishing the case for Swinburne as the greatest nineteenth-century English poet of sexual desire.

\* \* \*

*Poems and Ballads* was predictably a sensation. There are stories of Oxford undergraduates marching arm in arm down the High Street chanting 'Dolores', and the book went through some forty editions by the end of the century. Swinburne's poetry (and criticism) was a crucial influence on the English Aesthetic movement (Pater cited him as font for his own impressionistic criticism), and after that the 'decadent' poets of the *fin de siècle*—Ernest Dowson, Lionel Johnson, Oscar Wilde, and others. In his specifically erotic mode, Swinburne provided striking embodiments of a range of themes—the consuming *femme fatale*, the polymorphism of sexual desire, the compelling nexus of pleasure and pain—that would become common currency of turn-of-the-century art and writing both in England and the Continent.

He was read throughout Europe: Stéphane Mallarmé admired his work greatly, as did Gabriele D'Annunzio and Stefan George. His work was especially inspiring for gay and lesbian poets such as 'Michael Field' (Katherine Harris Bradley and Edith Emma Cooper) and, somewhat later, H.D. (Hilda Doolittle). Among twentieth-century English-language poets, Edith Sitwell was most unreserved in her praise of Swinburne, but marks of his influence are clear in the works of Ezra Pound, W.H. Auden, and even the Doubting Thomas, Eliot. Unlike Gerard Manley Hopkins or Robert Browning, it is difficult to make a case for Swinburne as a proto-modernist—certainly not in terms of forms and diction. But taken on its own terms, his poetry is a formidable and perversely fascinating accomplishment.

The editor extends thanks for information, aid, and encouragement to Robert Archambeau, Jean Callahan, Sally Connolly, Joseph Donahue, Norman Finkelstein, Warren Kelly, Catherine Maxwell, Marcella Munson, Eric Murphy Selinger, and Daniel Tiffany.

# Further Reading

Until the publication of a five-volume collection of Swinburne's *Poetical Works* (announced by Routledge for the end of 2019) under the editorship of Tim Burnett, Charles L. Sligh, and John Walsh, the 1904 six-volume Chatto & Windus edition of Swinburne's poems remains definitive. The texts of the 1925-1927 "Bonchurch Edition" (twenty volumes, edited by Edmund Gosse and T. J. Wise), are unreliable, though that edition does present poems uncollected in 1904. There have been a number of modern selections of Swinburne, best among them *Major Poems and Selected Prose*, edited by Jerome J. McGann and Charles L. Sligh (Yale University Press, 2004), *Selected Verse*, edited by Alex Wong (Carcanet Press, 2015), and the comprehensive Oxford 21st-Century Authors *Algernon Charles Swinburne*, edited by Francis O'Gorman (2017). Kenneth Haynes has edited *Poems and Ballads & Atalanta in Calydon* for Penguin (2000). Cecil Y. Lang's *The Swinburne Letters* (six volumes, Yale University Press, 1959-1962) is essential; Swinburne's public statements on his own work are presented in *Swinburne Replies: Notes on Poems and Review; Under the Microscope; Dedicatory Epistle*, edited by Clyde K. Hyder (Syracuse University Press, 1966). Of the numerous biographies, the most recent, Rikky Rooksby's *A. C. Swinburne: A Poet's Life* (Scolar Press, 1997) is the most lively and readable. Swinburne's contemporary critical rehabilitation began with John D. Rosenberg's "Swinburne" (*Victorian Studies* 11.2, December 1967), which has been followed by a number of critical studies, of which Jerome J. McGann's *Swinburne: An Experiment in Criticism* (University of Chicago Press, 1972) remains by far the finest and most comprehensive.

# A Note on the Texts

Most of the poems here are reproduced in the texts included in the 1904 Chatto & Windus edition of Swinburne's poems, the last produced under the poet's direct supervision. The final three lines of stanza VII and the sixth line of stanza IX of 'The Complaint of the Fair Armouress' were replaced with asterisks in 1904; modern editors restore these lines from posthumous editions published by Thomas J. Wise. The passage from *Chastelard* is taken from Volume II of *Swinburne's Tragedies* (Chatto & Windus, 1905). 'Cleopatra' was first published in 1866 in *The Cornhill*, but was not included in Swinburne's collected poems until the impression of 1912; that text (from volume VI) is followed here. The text of 'Pasiphae' is from Catherine Maxwell's transcription of the draft manuscript, published in her *Swinburne* (Tavistock: Northcote House, 2006); I am very grateful for her kind permission to reproduce her work here.

# from *Chastelard: A Tragedy* (Act V, scene ii)

CHASTELARD
So here my time shuts up; and the last light
Has made the last shade in the world for me.
The sunbeam that was narrow like a leaf
Has turned a hand, and the hand stretched to an arm,
And the arm has reached the dust on the floor, and made
A maze of motes with paddling fingers. Well,
I knew not that a man so sure to die
Could care so little; a bride-night's lustiness
Leaps in my veins as light fire under a wind:
As if I felt a kindling beyond death   10
Of some new joys far outside of me yet;
Sweet sound, sweet smell and touch of things far out
Sure to come soon. I wonder will death be
Even all it seems now? or the talk of hell
And wretched changes of the worn-out soul
Nailed to decaying flesh, shall that be true?
Or is this like the forethought of deep sleep
Felt by a tired man? Sleep were good enough—
Shall sleep be all? But I shall not forget
For any sleep this love bound upon me—   20
For any sleep or quiet ways of death.
Ah, in my weary dusty space of sight
Her face will float with heavy scents of hair
And fire of subtle amorous eyes, and lips
More hot than wine, full of sweet wicked words
Babbled against mine own lips, and long hands
Spread out, and pale bright throat and pale bright breasts,
Fit to make all men mad. I do believe
This fire shall never quite burn out to the ash
And leave no heat and flame upon my dust   30
For witness where a man's heart was burnt up.
For all Christ's work this Venus is not quelled,
But reddens at the mouth with blood of men,
Sucking between small teeth the sap o' the veins,
Dabbling with death her little tender lips—

A bitter beauty, poisonous-pearlèd mouth.
I am not fit to live but for love's sake,
So I were best die shortly. Ah, fair love,
Fair fearful Venus made of deadly foam,
I shall escape you somehow with my death—  40
Your splendid supple body and mouth on fire
And Paphian breath that bites the lips with heat.
I had best die.

# A Ballad of Life

I found in dreams a place of wind and flowers,
    Full of sweet trees and colour of glad grass,
      In midst whereof there was
A lady clothed like summer with sweet hours.
Her beauty, fervent as a fiery moon,
    Made my blood burn and swoon
      Like a flame rained upon.
Sorrow had filled her shaken eyelids' blue,
And her mouth's sad red heavy rose all through
    Seemed sad with glad things gone.          10

She held a little cithern by the strings,
    Shaped heartwise, strung with subtle-coloured hair
      Of some dead lute-player
That in dead years had done delicious things.
The seven strings were named accordingly;
    The first string charity,
      The second tenderness,
The rest were pleasure, sorrow, sleep, and sin,
And loving-kindness, that is pity's kin
    And is most pitiless.          20

There were three men with her, each garmented
    With gold and shod with gold upon the feet;
      And with plucked ears of wheat
The first man's hair was wound upon his head:
His face was red, and his mouth curled and sad;
    All his gold garment had
      Pale stains of dust and rust.
A riven hood was pulled across his eyes;
The token of him being upon this wise
    Made for a sign of Lust.          30

The next was Shame, with hollow heavy face
    Coloured like green wood when flame kindles it.
      He hath such feeble feet

They may not well endure in any place.
His face was full of grey old miseries,
   And all his blood's increase
     Was even increase of pain.
The last was Fear, that is akin to Death;
He is Shame's friend, and always as Shame saith
     Fear answers him again.                      40

My soul said in me; This is marvellous,
   Seeing the air's face is not so delicate
   Nor the sun's grace so great,
If sin and she be kin or amorous.
And seeing where maidens served her on their knees,
   I bade one crave of these
     To know the cause thereof.
Then Fear said: I am Pity that was dead.
And Shame said: I am Sorrow comforted.
     And Lust said: I am Love.                      50

Thereat her hands began a lute-playing
   And her sweet mouth a song in a strange tongue;
   And all the while she sung
There was no sound but long tears following
Long tears upon men's faces, waxen white
   With extreme sad delight.
     But those three following men
Became as men raised up among the dead;
Great glad mouths open and fair cheeks made red
     With child's blood come again.                60

Then I said: Now assuredly I see
   My lady is perfect, and transfigureth
   All sin and sorrow and death,
Making them fair as her own eyelids be,
Or lips wherein my whole soul's life abides;
   Or as her sweet white sides
     And bosom carved to kiss.
Now therefore, if her pity further me,
Doubtless for her sake all my days shall be
     As righteous as she is.                      70

Forth, ballad, and take roses in both arms,
   Even till the top rose touch thee in the throat
Where the least thornprick harms;
   And girdled in thy golden singing-coat,
Come thou before my lady and say this;
   Borgia, thy gold hair's colour burns in me,
     Thy mouth makes beat my blood in feverish rhymes;
   Therefore so many as these roses be,
     Kiss me so many times.
Then it may be, seeing how sweet she is,          80
   That she will stoop herself none otherwise
     Than a blown vine-branch doth,
   And kiss thee with soft laughter on thine eyes,
     Ballad, and on thy mouth.

## Laus Veneris

Lors dit en plourant; Hélas trop malheureux homme et mauldict pescheur, oncques ne verrai-je clémence et miséricorde de Dieu. Ores m'en irai-je d'icy et me cacherai dedans le mont Horsel, en requérant de faveur et d'amoureuse merci ma doulce dame Vénus, car pour son amour serai-je bien à tout jamais damné en enfer. Voicy la fin de tous mes faicts d'armes et de toutes mes belles chansons. Hélas, trop belle estoyt la face de ma dame et ses yeulx, et en mauvais jour je vis ces chouses-là. Lors s'en alla tout en gémissant et se retourna chez elle, et là vescut tristement en grand amour près de sa dame. Puis après advint que le pape vit un jour esclater sur son baston force belles fleurs rouges et blanches et maints boutons de feuilles, et ainsi vit-il reverdir toute l'escorce. Ce dont il eut grande crainte et moult s'en esmut, et grande pitié lui prit de ce chevalier qui s'en estoyt départi sans espoir comme un homme misérable et damné. Doncques envoya force messaigers devers luy pour le ramener, disant qu'il aurait de Dieu grace et bonne absolution de son grand pesché d'amour. Mais oncques plus ne le virent; car toujours demeura ce pauvre chevalier auprès de Vénus la haulte et forte déesse ès flancs de la montagne amoureuse.

> *Livre des grandes merveilles d'amour,*
> *escript en latin et en françoys par*
> *Maistre Antoine Gaget.* 1530.

## Laus Veneris

Asleep or waking is it? for her neck,
Kissed over close, wears yet a purple speck
   Wherein the pained blood falters and goes out;
Soft, and stung softly—fairer for a fleck.

But though my lips shut sucking on the place,
There is no vein at work upon her face;
   Her eyelids are so peaceable, no doubt
Deep sleep has warmed her blood through all its ways.

Lo, this is she that was the world's delight;
The old grey years were parcels of her might;     10
   The strewings of the ways wherein she trod
Were the twain seasons of the day and night.

Lo, she was thus when her clear limbs enticed
All lips that now grow sad with kissing Christ,
    Stained with blood fallen from the feet of God,
The feet and hands whereat our souls were priced.

Alas, Lord, surely thou art great and fair.
But lo her wonderfully woven hair!
    And thou didst heal us with thy piteous kiss;
But see now, Lord; her mouth is lovelier.

She is right fair; what hath she done to thee?
Nay, fair Lord Christ, lift up thine eyes and see;
    Had now thy mother such a lip — like this?
Thou knowest how sweet a thing it is to me.

Inside the Horsel here the air is hot;
Right little peace one hath for it, God wot;
    The scented dusty daylight burns the air,
And my heart chokes me till I hear it not.

Behold, my Venus, my soul's body, lies
With my love laid upon her garment-wise,
    Feeling my love in all her limbs and hair
And shed between her eyelids through her eyes.

She holds my heart in her sweet open hands
Hanging asleep; hard by her head there stands,
    Crowned with gilt thorns and clothed with flesh like fire,
Love, wan as foam blown up the salt burnt sands—

Hot as the brackish waifs of yellow spume
That shift and steam—loose clots of arid fume
    From the sea's panting mouth of dry desire;
There stands he, like one labouring at a loom.

The warp holds fast across; and every thread
That makes the woof up has dry specks of red;
    Always the shuttle cleaves clean through, and he
Weaves with the hair of many a ruined head.

Love is not glad nor sorry, as I deem;
Labouring he dreams, and labours in the dream,
   Till when the spool is finished, lo I see
His web, reeled off, curls and goes out like steam.

Night falls like fire; the heavy lights run low,
And as they drop, my blood and body so 50
   Shake as the flame shakes, full of days and hours
That sleep not neither weep they as they go.

Ah yet would God this flesh of mine might be
Where air might wash and long leaves cover me,
   Where tides of grass break into foam of flowers,
Or where the wind's feet shine along the sea.

Ah yet would God that stems and roots were bred
Out of my weary body and my head,
   That sleep were sealed upon me with a seal,
And I were as the least of all his dead. 60

Would God my blood were dew to feed the grass,
Mine ears made deaf and mine eyes blind as glass,
   My body broken as a turning wheel,
And my mouth stricken ere it saith Alas!

Ah God, that love were as a flower or flame,
That life were as the naming of a name,
   That death were not more pitiful than desire,
That these things were not one thing and the same!

Behold now, surely somewhere there is death:
For each man hath some space of years, he saith, 70
   A little space of time ere time expire,
A little day, a little way of breath.

And lo, between the sundawn and the sun,
His day's work and his night's work are undone;
   And lo, between the nightfall and the light,
He is not, and none knoweth of such an one.

Ah God, that I were as all souls that be,
As any herb or leaf of any tree,
    As men that toil through hours of labouring night,
As bones of men under the deep sharp sea.                                 80

Outside it must be winter among men;
For at the gold bars of the gates again
    I heard all night and all the hours of it
The wind's wet wings and fingers drip with rain.

Knights gather, riding sharp for cold; I know
The ways and woods are strangled with the snow;
    And with short song the maidens spin and sit
Until Christ's birthnight, lily-like, arow.

The scent and shadow shed about me make
The very soul in all my senses ache;                                             90
    The hot hard night is fed upon my breath,
And sleep beholds me from afar awake.

Alas, but surely where the hills grow deep,
Or where the wild ways of the sea are steep,
    Or in strange places somewhere there is death,
And on death's face the scattered hair of sleep.

There lover-like with lips and limbs that meet
They lie, they pluck sweet fruit of life and eat;
    But me the hot and hungry days devour,
And in my mouth no fruit of theirs is sweet.                           100

No fruit of theirs, but fruit of my desire,
For her love's sake whose lips through mine respire;
    Her eyelids on her eyes like flower on flower,
Mine eyelids on mine eyes like fire on fire.

So lie we, not as sleep that lies by death,
With heavy kisses and with happy breath;
    Not as man lies by woman, when the bride
Laughs low for love's sake and the words he saith.

For she lies, laughing low with love; she lies
And turns his kisses on her lips to sighs, 110
   To sighing sound of lips unsatisfied,
And the sweet tears are tender with her eyes.

Ah, not as they, but as the souls that were
Slain in the old time, having found her fair;
   Who, sleeping with her lips upon their eyes,
Heard sudden serpents hiss across her hair.

Their blood runs round the roots of time like rain:
She casts them forth and gathers them again;
   With nerve and bone she weaves and multiplies
Exceeding pleasure out of extreme pain. 120

Her little chambers drip with flower-like red,
Her girdles, and the chaplets of her head,
   Her armlets and her anklets; with her feet
She tramples all that winepress of the dead.

Her gateways smoke with fume of flowers and fires,
With loves burnt out and unassuaged desires;
   Between her lips the steam of them is sweet,
The languor in her ears of many lyres.

Her beds are full of perfume and sad sound,
Her doors are made with music, and barred round 130
   With sighing and with laughter and with tears,
With tears whereby strong souls of men are bound.

There is the knight Adonis that was slain;
With flesh and blood she chains him for a chain;
   The body and the spirit in her ears
Cry, for her lips divide him vein by vein.

Yea, all she slayeth; yea, every man save me;
Me, love, thy lover that must cleave to thee
   Till the ending of the days and ways of earth,
The shaking of the sources of the sea. 140

Me, most forsaken of all souls that fell;
Me, satiated with things insatiable;
   Me, for whose sake the extreme hell makes mirth,
Yea, laughter kindles at the heart of hell.

Alas thy beauty! for thy mouth's sweet sake
My soul is bitter to me, my limbs quake
   As water, as the flesh of men that weep,
As their heart's vein whose heart goes nigh to break.

Ah God, that sleep with flower-sweet finger-tips
Would crush the fruit of death upon my lips;          150
   Ah God, that death would tread the grapes of sleep
And wring their juice upon me as it drips.

There is no change of cheer for many days,
But change of chimes high up in the air, that sways
   Rung by the running fingers of the wind;
And singing sorrows heard on hidden ways.

Day smiteth day in twain, night sundereth night,
And on mine eyes the dark sits as the light;
   Yea, Lord, thou knowest I know not, having sinned,
If heaven be clean or unclean in thy sight.              160

Yea, as if earth were sprinkled over me,
Such chafed harsh earth as chokes a sandy sea,
   Each pore doth yearn, and the dried blood thereof
Gasps by sick fits, my heart swims heavily,

There is a feverish famine in my veins;
Below her bosom, where a crushed grape stains
   The white and blue, there my lips caught and clove
An hour since, and what mark of me remains?

I dare not always touch her, lest the kiss
Leave my lips charred. Yea, Lord, a little bliss,        170
   Brief bitter bliss, one hath for a great sin;
Nathless thou knowest how sweet a thing it is.

Sin, is it sin whereby men's souls are thrust
Into the pit? yet had I a good trust
   To save my soul before it slipped therein,
Trod under by the fire-shod feet of lust.

For if mine eyes fail and my soul takes breath,
I look between the iron sides of death
   Into sad hell where all sweet love hath end,
All but the pain that never finisheth.                                180

There are the naked faces of great kings,
The singing folk with all their lute-playings;
   There when one cometh he shall have to friend
The grave that covets and the worm that clings.

There sit the knights that were so great of hand,
The ladies that were queens of fair green land,
   Grown grey and black now, brought unto the dust,
Soiled, without raiment, clad about with sand.

There is one end for all of them; they sit
Naked and sad, they drink the dregs of it,                         190
   Trodden as grapes in the wine-press of lust,
Trampled and trodden by the fiery feet.

I see the marvellous mouth whereby there fell
Cities and people whom the gods loved well,
   Yet for her sake on them the fire gat hold,
And for their sakes on her the fire of hell.

And softer than the Egyptian lote-leaf is,
The queen whose face was worth the world to kiss,
   Wearing at breast a suckling snake of gold;
And large pale lips of strong Semiramis,                       200

Curled like a tiger's that curl back to feed;
Red only where the last kiss made them bleed;
   Her hair most thick with many a carven gem,
Deep in the mane, great-chested, like a steed.

Yea, with red sin the faces of them shine;
But in all these there was no sin like mine;
   No, not in all the strange great sins of them
That made the wine-press froth and foam with wine.

For I was of Christ's choosing, I God's knight,
No blinkard heathen stumbling for scant light;
   I can well see, for all the dusty days
Gone past, the clean great time of goodly fight.

I smell the breathing battle sharp with blows,
With shriek of shafts and snapping short of bows;
   The fair pure sword smites out in subtle ways,
Sounds and long lights are shed between the rows

Of beautiful mailed men; the edged light slips,
Most like a snake that takes short breath and dips
   Sharp from the beautifully bending head,
With all its gracious body lithe as lips

That curl in touching you; right in this wise
My sword doth, seeming fire in mine own eyes,
   Leaving all colours in them brown and red
And flecked with death; then the keen breaths like sighs,

The caught-up choked dry laughters following them,
When all the fighting face is grown a flame
   For pleasure, and the pulse that stuns the ears,
And the heart's gladness of the goodly game.

Let me think yet a little; I do know
These things were sweet, but sweet such years ago,
   Their savour is all turned now into tears;
Yea, ten years since, where the blue ripples blow,

The blue curled eddies of the blowing Rhine,
I felt the sharp wind shaking grass and vine
   Touch my blood too, and sting me with delight
Through all this waste and weary body of mine

That never feels clear air; right gladly then
I rode alone, a great way off my men,
   And heard the chiming bridle smite and smite,
And gave each rhyme thereof some rhyme again,           240

Till my song shifted to that iron one;
Seeing there rode up between me and the sun
   Some certain of my foe's men, for his three
White wolves across their painted coats did run.

The first red-bearded, with square cheeks—alack,
I made my knave's blood turn his beard to black;
   The slaying of him was a joy to see:
Perchance too, when at night he came not back,

Some woman fell a-weeping, whom this thief
Would beat when he had drunken; yet small grief         250
   Hath any for the ridding of such knaves;
Yea, if one wept, I doubt her teen was brief.

This bitter love is sorrow in all lands,
Draining of eyelids, wringing of drenched hands,
   Sighing of hearts and filling up of graves;
A sign across the head of the world he stands,

An one that hath a plague-mark on his brows;
Dust and spilt blood do track him to his house
   Down under earth; sweet smells of lip and cheek,
Like a sweet snake's breath made more poisonous       260

With chewing of some perfumed deadly grass,
Are shed all round his passage if he pass,
   And their quenched savour leaves the whole soul weak,
Sick with keen guessing whence the perfume was.

As one who hidden in deep sedge and reeds
Smells the rare scent made where a panther feeds,
   And tracking ever slotwise the warm smell
Is snapped upon by the sweet mouth and bleeds,

His head far down the hot sweet throat of her—
So one tracks love, whose breath is deadlier,
   And lo, one springe and you are fast in hell,
Fast as the gin's grip of a wayfarer.

I think now, as the heavy hours decease
One after one, and bitter thoughts increase
   One upon one, of all sweet finished things;
The breaking of the battle; the long peace

Wherein we sat clothed softly, each man's hair
Crowned with green leaves beneath white hoods of vair;
   The sounds of sharp spears at great tourneyings,
And noise of singing in the late sweet air.

I sang of love too, knowing nought thereof;
"Sweeter," I said, "the little laugh of love
   Than tears out of the eyes of Magdalen,
Or any fallen feather of the Dove.

"The broken little laugh that spoils a kiss,
The ache of purple pulses, and the bliss
   Of blinded eyelids that expand again—
Love draws them open with those lips of his,

"Lips that cling hard till the kissed face has grown
Of one same fire and colour with their own;
   Then ere one sleep, appeased with sacrifice,
Where his lips wounded, there his lips atone."

I sang these things long since and knew them not;
"Lo, here is love, or there is love, God wot,
   This man and that finds favour in his eyes,"
I said, "but I, what guerdon have I got?

"The dust of praise that is blown everywhere
In all men's faces with the common air;
   The bay-leaf that wants chafing to be sweet
Before they wind it in a singer's hair."

So that one dawn I rode forth sorrowing;
I had no hope but of some evil thing,
   And so rode slowly past the windy wheat
And past the vineyard and the water-spring,

Up to the Horsel. A great elder-tree
Held back its heaps of flowers to let me see
   The ripe tall grass, and one that walked therein,
Naked, with hair shed over to the knee.

She walked between the blossom and the grass;
I knew the beauty of her, what she was,                    310
   The beauty of her body and her sin,
And in my flesh the sin of hers, alas!

Alas! for sorrow is all the end of this.
O sad kissed mouth, how sorrowful it is!
   O breast whereat some suckling sorrow clings,
Red with the bitter blossom of a kiss!

Ah, with blind lips I felt for you, and found
About my neck your hands and hair enwound,
   The hands that stifle and the hair that stings,
I felt them fasten sharply without sound.                      320

Yea, for my sin I had great store of bliss:
Rise up, make answer for me, let thy kiss
   Seal my lips hard from speaking of my sin,
Lest one go mad to hear how sweet it is.

Yet I waxed faint with fume of barren bowers,
And murmuring of the heavy-headed hours;
   And let the dove's beak fret and peck within
My lips in vain, and Love shed fruitless flowers.

So that God looked upon me when your hands
Were hot about me; yea, God brake my bands            330
   To save my soul alive, and I came forth
Like a man blind and naked in strange lands

That hears men laugh and weep, and knows not whence
Nor wherefore, but is broken in his sense;
   Howbeit I met folk riding from the north
Towards Rome, to purge them of their souls' offence,

And rode with them, and spake to none; the day
Stunned me like lights upon some wizard way,
   And ate like fire mine eyes and mine eyesight;
So rode I, hearing all these chant and pray,                       340

And marvelled; till before us rose and fell
White cursed hills, like outer skirts of hell
   Seen where men's eyes look through the day to night,
Like a jagged shell's lips, harsh, untunable,

Blown in between by devils' wrangling breath;
Nathless we won well past that hell and death,
   Down to the sweet land where all airs are good,
Even unto Rome where God's grace tarrieth.

Then came each man and worshipped at his knees
Who in the Lord God's likeness bears the keys                       350
   To bind or loose, and called on Christ's shed blood,
And so the sweet-souled father gave him ease.

But when I came I fell down at his feet,
Saying, "Father, though the Lord's blood be right sweet,
   The spot it takes not off the panther's skin,
Nor shall an Ethiop's stain be bleached with it.

"Lo, I have sinned and have spat out at God,
Wherefore his hand is heavier and his rod
   More sharp because of mine exceeding sin,
And all his raiment redder than bright blood                      360

"Before mine eyes; yea, for my sake I wot
The heat of hell is waxen seven times hot
   Through my great sin." Then spake he some sweet word,
Giving me cheer; which thing availed me not;

Yea, scarce I wist if such indeed were said;
For when I ceased—lo, as one newly dead
   Who hears a great cry out of hell, I heard
The crying of his voice across my head.

"Until this dry shred staff, that hath no whit
Of leaf nor bark, bear blossom and smell sweet,           370
   Seek thou not any mercy in God's sight,
For so long shalt thou be cast out from it."

Yea, what if dried-up stems wax red and green,
Shall that thing be which is not nor has been?
   Yea, what if sapless bark wax green and white,
Shall any good fruit grow upon my sin?

Nay, though sweet fruit were plucked of a dry tree,
And though men drew sweet waters of the sea,
   There should not grow sweet leaves on this dead stem,
This waste wan body and shaken soul of me.           380

Yea, though God search it warily enough,
There is not one sound thing in all thereof;
   Though he search all my veins through, searching them
He shall find nothing whole therein but love.

For I came home right heavy, with small cheer,
And lo my love, mine own soul's heart, more dear
   Than mine own soul, more beautiful than God,
Who hath my being between the hands of her—

Fair still, but fair for no man saving me,
As when she came out of the naked sea           390
   Making the foam as fire whereon she trod,
And as the inner flower of fire was she.

Yea, she laid hold upon me, and her mouth
Clove unto mine as soul to body doth,
   And, laughing, made her lips luxurious;
Her hair had smells of all the sunburnt south,

Strange spice and flower, strange savour of crushed fruit,
And perfume the swart kings tread underfoot
   For pleasure when their minds wax amorous,
Charred frankincense and grated sandal-root.                      400

And I forgot fear and all weary things,
All ended prayers and perished thanksgivings,
   Feeling her face with all her eager hair
Cleave to me, clinging as a fire that clings

To the body and to the raiment, burning them;
As after death I know that such-like flame
   Shall cleave to me for ever; yea, what care,
Albeit I burn then, having felt the same?

Ah love, there is no better life than this;
To have known love, how bitter a thing it is,                           410
   And afterward be cast out of God's sight;
Yea, these that know not, shall they have such bliss

High up in barren heaven before his face
As we twain in the heavy-hearted place,
   Remembering love and all the dead delight,
And all that time was sweet with for a space?

For till the thunder in the trumpet be,
Soul may divide from body, but not we
   One from another; I hold thee with my hand,
I let mine eyes have all their will of thee,                               420

I seal myself upon thee with my might,
Abiding alway out of all men's sight
   Until God loosen over sea and land
The thunder of the trumpets of the night.

EXPLICIT LAUS VENERIS.

## Les Noyades

Whatever a man of the sons of men
    Shall say to his heart of the lords above,
They have shown man verily, once and again,
    Marvellous mercies and infinite love.

In the wild fifth year of the change of things,
    When France was glorious and blood-red, fair
With dust of battle and deaths of kings,
    A queen of men, with helmeted hair,

Carrier came down to the Loire and slew,
    Till all the ways and the waves waxed red:
Bound and drowned, slaying two by two,
    Maidens and young men, naked and wed.

They brought on a day to his judgment-place
    One rough with labour and red with fight,
And a lady noble by name and face,
    Faultless, a maiden, wonderful, white.

She knew not, being for shame's sake blind,
    If his eyes were hot on her face hard by.
And the judge bade strip and ship them, and bind
    Bosom to bosom, to drown and die.

The white girl winced and whitened; but he
    Caught fire, waxed bright as a great bright flame
Seen with thunder far out on the sea,
    Laughed hard as the glad blood went and came.

Twice his lips quailed with delight, then said,
    "I have but a word to you all, one word;
Bear with me; surely I am but dead;"
    And all they laughed and mocked him and heard.

"Judge, when they open the judgment-roll,
    I will stand upright before God and pray:
'Lord God, have mercy on one man's soul,
    For his mercy was great upon earth, I say.

"'Lord, if I loved thee—Lord, if I served—
    If these who darkened thy fair Son's face
I fought with, sparing not one, nor swerved
    A hand's-breadth, Lord, in the perilous place—

"'I pray thee say to this man, O Lord,
    *Sit thou for him at my feet on a throne.*
I will face thy wrath, though it bite as a sword,
    And my soul shall burn for his soul, and atone.

"'For, Lord, thou knowest, O God most wise,
    How gracious on earth were his deeds towards me.
Shall this be a small thing in thine eyes,
    That is greater in mine than the whole great sea?'

"I have loved this woman my whole life long,
    And even for love's sake when have I said
'I love you'? when have I done you wrong,
    Living? but now I shall have you dead.

"Yea, now, do I bid you love me, love?
    Love me or loathe, we are one not twain.
But God be praised in his heaven above
    For this my pleasure and that my pain!

"For never a man, being mean like me,
    Shall die like me till the whole world dies.
I shall drown with her, laughing for love; and she
    Mix with me, touching me, lips and eyes.

"Shall she not know me and see me all through,
    Me, on whose heart as a worm she trod?
You have given me, God requite it you,
    What man yet never was given of God."

O sweet one love, O my life's delight,
   Dear, though the days have divided us,
Lost beyond hope, taken far out of sight,
   Not twice in the world shall the gods do thus.

Had it been so hard for my love? but I,
   Though the gods gave all that a god can give,
I had chosen rather the gift to die,
   Cease, and be glad above all that live.

For the Loire would have driven us down to the sea,
   And the sea would have pitched us from shoal to shoal;      70
And I should have held you, and you held me,
   As flesh holds flesh, and the soul the soul.

Could I change you, help you to love me, sweet,
   Could I give you the love that would sweeten death,
We should yield, go down, locked hands and feet,
   Die, drown together, and breath catch breath;

But you would have felt my soul in a kiss,
   And known that once if I loved you well;
And I would have given my soul for this
   To burn for ever in burning hell.

# Anactoria

> τίνος αὖ τὺ πειθοῖ
> μὰψ σαγηνεύσας φιλότατα;
> > SAPPHO.

My life is bitter with thy love; thine eyes
Blind me, thy tresses burn me, thy sharp sighs
Divide my flesh and spirit with soft sound,
And my blood strengthens, and my veins abound.
I pray thee sigh not, speak not, draw not breath;
Let life burn down, and dream it is not death.
I would the sea had hidden us, the fire
(Wilt thou fear that, and fear not my desire?)
Severed the bones that bleach, the flesh that cleaves,
And let our sifted ashes drop like leaves.     10
I feel thy blood against my blood: my pain
Pains thee, and lips bruise lips, and vein stings vein.
Let fruit be crushed on fruit, let flower on flower,
Breast kindle breast, and either burn one hour.
Why wilt thou follow lesser loves? are thine
Too weak to bear these hands and lips of mine?
I charge thee for my life's sake, O too sweet
To crush love with thy cruel faultless feet,
I charge thee keep thy lips from hers or his,
Sweetest, till theirs be sweeter than my kiss:     20
Lest I too lure, a swallow for a dove,
Erotion or Erinna to my love.
I would my love could kill thee; I am satiated
With seeing thee live, and fain would have thee dead.
I would earth had thy body as fruit to eat,
And no mouth but some serpent's found thee sweet.
I would find grievous ways to have thee slain,
Intense device, and superflux of pain;
Vex thee with amorous agonies, and shake
Life at thy lips, and leave it there to ache;     30
Strain out thy soul with pangs too soft to kill,
Intolerable interludes, and infinite ill;
Relapse and reluctation of the breath,

Dumb tunes and shuddering semitones of death.
I am weary of all thy words and soft strange ways,
Of all love's fiery nights and all his days,
And all the broken kisses salt as brine
That shuddering lips make moist with waterish wine,
And eyes the bluer for all those hidden hours
That pleasure fills with tears and feeds from flowers, 40
Fierce at the heart with fire that half comes through,
But all the flowerlike white stained round with blue;
The fervent underlid, and that above
Lifted with laughter or abashed with love;
Thine amorous girdle, full of thee and fair,
And leavings of the lilies in thine hair.
Yea, all sweet words of thine and all thy ways,
And all the fruit of nights and flower of days,
And stinging lips wherein the hot sweet brine
That Love was born of burns and foams like wine, 50
And eyes insatiable of amorous hours,
Fervent as fire and delicate as flowers,
Coloured like night at heart, but cloven through
Like night with flame, dyed round like night with blue,
Clothed with deep eyelids under and above—
Yea, all thy beauty sickens me with love;
Thy girdle empty of thee and now not fair,
And ruinous lilies in thy languid hair.
Ah, take no thought for Love's sake; shall this be,
And she who loves thy lover not love thee? 60
Sweet soul, sweet mouth of all that laughs and lives,
Mine is she, very mine; and she forgives.
For I beheld in sleep the light that is
In her high place in Paphos, heard the kiss
Of body and soul that mix with eager tears
And laughter stinging through the eyes and ears;
Saw Love, as burning flame from crown to feet,
Imperishable, upon her storied seat;
Clear eyelids lifted toward the north and south,
A mind of many colours, and a mouth 70
Of many tunes and kisses; and she bowed,
With all her subtle face laughing aloud,

Bowed down upon me, saying, "Who doth thee wrong,
Sappho?" but thou—thy body is the song,
Thy mouth the music; thou art more than I,
Though my voice die not till the whole world die;
Though men that hear it madden; though love weep,
Though nature change, though shame be charmed to sleep.
Ah, wilt thou slay me lest I kiss thee dead?
Yet the queen laughed from her sweet heart and said: 80
"Even she that flies shall follow for thy sake,
And she shall give thee gifts that would not take,
Shall kiss that would not kiss thee" (yea, kiss me)
"When thou wouldst not" — when I would not kiss thee!
Ah, more to me than all men as thou art,
Shall not my songs assuage her at the heart?
Ah, sweet to me as life seems sweet to death,
Why should her wrath fill thee with fearful breath?
Nay, sweet, for is she God alone? hath she
Made earth and all the centuries of the sea, 90
Taught the sun ways to travel, woven most fine
The moonbeams, shed the starbeams forth as wine,
Bound with her myrtles, beaten with her rods,
The young men and the maidens and the gods?
Have we not lips to love with, eyes for tears,
And summer and flower of women and of years?
Stars for the foot of morning, and for noon
Sunlight, and exaltation of the moon;
Waters that answer waters, fields that wear
Lilies, and languor of the Lesbian air? 100
Beyond those flying feet of fluttered doves,
Are there not other gods for other loves?
Yea, though she scourge thee, sweetest, for my sake,
Blossom not thorns and flowers not blood should break.
Ah that my lips were tuneless lips, but pressed
To the bruised blossom of thy scourged white breast!
Ah that my mouth for Muses' milk were fed
On the sweet blood thy sweet small wounds had bled!
That with my tongue I felt them, and could taste
The faint flakes from thy bosom to the waist! 110
That I could drink thy veins as wine, and eat

Thy breasts like honey! that from face to feet
Thy body were abolished and consumed,
And in my flesh thy very flesh entombed!
Ah, ah, thy beauty! like a beast it bites,
Stings like an adder, like an arrow smites.
Ah sweet, and sweet again, and seven times sweet,
The paces and the pauses of thy feet!
Ah sweeter than all sleep or summer air
The fallen fillets fragrant from thine hair!  120
Yea, though their alien kisses do me wrong,
Sweeter thy lips than mine with all their song;
Thy shoulders whiter than a fleece of white,
And flower-sweet fingers, good to bruise or bite
As honeycomb of the inmost honey-cells,
With almond-shaped and roseleaf-coloured shells
And blood like purple blossom at the tips
Quivering; and pain made perfect in thy lips
For my sake when I hurt thee; O that I
Durst crush thee out of life with love, and die,  130
Die of thy pain and my delight, and be
Mixed with thy blood and molten into thee!
Would I not plague thee dying overmuch?
Would I not hurt thee perfectly? not touch
Thy pores of sense with torture, and make bright
Thine eyes with bloodlike tears and grievous light?
Strike pang from pang as note is struck from note,
Catch the sob's middle music in thy throat,
Take thy limbs living, and new-mould with these
A lyre of many faultless agonies?  140
Feed thee with fever and famine and fine drouth,
With perfect pangs convulse thy perfect mouth,
Make thy life shudder in thee and burn afresh,
And wring thy very spirit through the flesh?
Cruel? but love makes all that love him well
As wise as heaven and crueller than hell.
Me hath love made more bitter toward thee
Than death toward man; but were I made as he
Who hath made all things to break them one by one,
If my feet trod upon the stars and sun  150

And souls of men as his have alway trod,
God knows I might be crueller than God.
For who shall change with prayers or thanksgivings
The mystery of the cruelty of things?
Or say what God above all gods and years
With offering and blood-sacrifice of tears,
With lamentation from strange lands, from graves
Where the snake pastures, from scarred mouths of slaves,
From prison, and from plunging prows of ships
Through flamelike foam of the sea's closing lips—    160
With thwartings of strange signs, and wind-blown hair
Of comets, desolating the dim air,
When darkness is made fast with seals and bars,
And fierce reluctance of disastrous stars,
Eclipse, and sound of shaken hills, and wings
Darkening, and blind inexpiable things—
With sorrow of labouring moons, and altering light
And travail of the planets of the night,
And weeping of the weary Pleiads seven,
Feeds the mute melancholy lust of heaven?    170
Is not his incense bitterness, his meat
Murder? his hidden face and iron feet
Hath not man known, and felt them on their way
Threaten and trample all things and every day?
Hath he not sent us hunger? who hath cursed
Spirit and flesh with longing? filled with thirst
Their lips who cried unto him? who bade exceed
The fervid will, fall short the feeble deed,
Bade sink the spirit and the flesh aspire,
Pain animate the dust of dead desire,    180
And life yield up her flower to violent fate?
Him would I reach, him smite, him desecrate,
Pierce the cold lips of God with human breath,
And mix his immortality with death.
Why hath he made us? what had all we done
That we should live and loathe the sterile sun,
And with the moon wax paler as she wanes,
And pulse by pulse feel time grow through our veins?
Thee too the years shall cover; thou shalt be

As the rose born of one same blood with thee, 190
As a song sung, as a word said, and fall
Flower-wise, and be not any more at all,
Nor any memory of thee anywhere;
For never Muse has bound above thine hair
The high Pierian flower whose graft outgrows
All summer kinship of the mortal rose
And colour of deciduous days, nor shed
Reflex and flush of heaven about thine head,
Nor reddened brows made pale by floral grief
With splendid shadow from that lordlier leaf. 200
Yea, thou shalt be forgotten like spilt wine,
Except these kisses of my lips on thine
Brand them with immortality; but me—
Men shall not see bright fire nor hear the sea,
Nor mix their hearts with music, nor behold
Cast forth of heaven, with feet of awful gold
And plumeless wings that make the bright air blind,
Lightning, with thunder for a hound behind
Hunting through fields unfurrowed and unsown,
But in the light and laughter, in the moan 210
And music, and in grasp of lip and hand
And shudder of water that makes felt on land
The immeasurable tremor of all the sea,
Memories shall mix and metaphors of me.
Like me shall be the shuddering calm of night,
When all the winds of the world for pure delight
Close lips that quiver and fold up wings that ache;
When nightingales are louder for love's sake,
And leaves tremble like lute-strings or like fire;
Like me the one star swooning with desire 220
Even at the cold lips of the sleepless moon,
As I at thine; like me the waste white noon,
Burnt through with barren sunlight; and like me
The land-stream and the tide-stream in the sea.
I am sick with time as these with ebb and flow,
And by the yearning in my veins I know
The yearning sound of waters; and mine eyes
Burn as that beamless fire which fills the skies

With troubled stars and travailing things of flame;
And in my heart the grief consuming them         230
Labours, and in my veins the thirst of these,
And all the summer travail of the trees
And all the winter sickness; and the earth,
Filled full with deadly works of death and birth,
Sore spent with hungry lusts of birth and death,
Has pain like mine in her divided breath;
Her spring of leaves is barren, and her fruit
Ashes; her boughs are burdened, and her root
Fibrous and gnarled with poison; underneath
Serpents have gnawn it through with tortuous teeth      240
Made sharp upon the bones of all the dead,
And wild birds rend her branches overhead.
These, woven as raiment for his word and thought,
These hath God made, and me as these, and wrought
Song, and hath lit it at my lips; and me
Earth shall not gather though she feed on thee.
As a shed tear shalt thou be shed; but I—
Lo, earth may labour, men live long and die,
Years change and stars, and the high God devise
New things, and old things wane before his eyes      250
Who wields and wrecks them, being more strong than they—
But, having made me, me he shall not slay.
Nor slay nor satiate, like those herds of his
Who laugh and live a little, and their kiss
Contents them, and their loves are swift and sweet,
And sure death grasps and gains them with slow feet,
Love they or hate they, strive or bow their knees—
And all these end; he hath his will of these.
Yea, but albeit he slay me, hating me—
Albeit he hide me in the deep dear sea              260
And cover me with cool wan foam, and ease
This soul of mine as any soul of these,
And give me water and great sweet waves, and make
The very sea's name lordlier for my sake,
The whole sea sweeter—albeit I die indeed
And hide myself and sleep and no man heed,
Of me the high God hath not all his will.

Blossom of branches, and on each high hill
Clear air and wind, and under in clamorous vales
Fierce noises of the fiery nightingales, 270
Buds burning in the sudden spring like fire,
The wan washed sand and the waves' vain desire,
Sails seen like blown white flowers at sea, and words
That bring tears swiftest, and long notes of birds
Violently singing till the whole world sings—
I Sappho shall be one with all these things,
With all high things for ever; and my face
Seen once, my songs once heard in a strange place,
Cleave to men's lives, and waste the days thereof
With gladness and much sadness and long love. 280
Yea, they shall say, earth's womb has borne in vain
New things, and never this best thing again;
Borne days and men, borne fruits and wars and wine,
Seasons and songs, but no song more like mine.
And they shall know me as ye who have known me here,
Last year when I loved Atthis, and this year
When I love thee; and they shall praise me, and say
"She hath all time as all we have our day,
Shall she not live and have her will"—even I?
Yea, though thou diest, I say I shall not die. 290
For these shall give me of their souls, shall give
Life, and the days and loves wherewith I live,
Shall quicken me with loving, fill with breath,
Save me and serve me, strive for me with death.
Alas, that neither moon nor snow nor dew
Nor all cold things can purge me wholly through,
Assuage me nor allay me nor appease,
Till supreme sleep shall bring me bloodless ease;
Till time wax faint in all his periods;
Till fate undo the bondage of the gods, 300
And lay, to slake and satiate me all through,
Lotus and Lethe on my lips like dew,
And shed around and over and under me
Thick darkness and the insuperable sea.

# Hermaphroditus

I
Lift up thy lips, turn round, look back for love,
    Blind love that comes by night and casts out rest;
    Of all things tired thy lips look weariest,
Save the long smile that they are wearied of.
Ah sweet, albeit no love be sweet enough,
    Choose of two loves and cleave unto the best;
    Two loves at either blossom of thy breast
Strive until one be under and one above.
Their breath is fire upon the amorous air,
    Fire in thine eyes and where thy lips suspire:     10
And whosoever hath seen thee, being so fair,
    Two things turn all his life and blood to fire;
A strong desire begot on great despair,
    A great despair cast out by strong desire.

II
Where between sleep and life some brief space is,
    With love like gold bound round about the head,
    Sex to sweet sex with lips and limbs is wed,
Turning the fruitful feud of hers and his
To the waste wedlock of a sterile kiss;
    Yet from them something like as fire is shed     20
    That shall not be assuaged till death be dead,
Though neither life nor sleep can find out this.
Love made himself of flesh that perisheth
    A pleasure-house for all the loves his kin;
But on the one side sat a man like death,
    And on the other a woman sat like sin.
So with veiled eyes and sobs between his breath
    Love turned himself and would not enter in.

III
Love, is it love or sleep or shadow or light
    That lies between thine eyelids and thine eyes?     30
    Like a flower laid upon a flower it lies,

Or like the night's dew laid upon the night.
Love stands upon thy left hand and thy right,
   Yet by no sunset and by no moonrise
     Shall make thee man and ease a woman's sighs,
Or make thee woman for a man's delight.
To what strange end hath some strange god made fair
     The double blossom of two fruitless flowers?
Hid love in all the folds of all thy hair,
   Fed thee on summers, watered thee with showers,      40
Given all the gold that all the seasons wear
   To thee that art a thing of barren hours?

IV
Yea, love, I see; it is not love but fear.
   Nay, sweet, it is not fear but love, I know;
     Or wherefore should thy body's blossom blow
So sweetly, or thine eyelids leave so clear
Thy gracious eyes that never made a tear —
     Though for their love our tears like blood should flow,
     Though love and life and death should come and go,
So dreadful, so desirable, so dear?      50
Yea, sweet, I know; I saw in what swift wise
   Beneath the woman's and the water's kiss
     Thy moist limbs melted into Salmacis,
And the large light turned tender in thine eyes,
And all thy boy's breath softened into sighs;
   But Love being blind, how should he know of this?

                 *Au Musée du Louvre, Mars* 1863.

# Fragoletta

O Love! what shall be said of thee?
The son of grief begot by joy?
Being sightless, wilt thou see?
Being sexless, wilt thou be
Maiden or boy?

I dreamed of strange lips yesterday
And cheeks wherein the ambiguous blood
Was like a rose's—yea,
A rose's when it lay
Within the bud.                                               10

What fields have bred thee, or what groves
Concealed thee, O mysterious flower,
O double rose of Love's,
With leaves that lure the doves
From bud to bower?

I dare not kiss it, lest my lip
Press harder than an indrawn breath,
And all the sweet life slip
Forth, and the sweet leaves drip,
Bloodlike, in death.                                          20

O sole desire of my delight!
O sole delight of my desire!
Mine eyelids and eyesight
Feed on thee day and night
Like lips of fire.

Lean back thy throat of carven pearl,
Let thy mouth murmur like the dove's;
Say, Venus hath no girl,
No front of female curl,
Among her Loves.                                              30

Thy sweet low bosom, thy close hair,
Thy strait soft flanks and slenderer feet,
Thy virginal strange air,
Are these not over fair
For Love to greet?

How should he greet thee? what new name,
Fit to move all men's hearts, could move
Thee, deaf to love or shame,
Love's sister, by the same
Mother as Love?                                              40

Ah sweet, the maiden's mouth is cold,
Her breast-blossoms are simply red,
Her hair mere brown or gold,
Fold over simple fold
Binding her head.

Thy mouth is made of fire and wine,
Thy barren bosom takes my kiss
And turns my soul to thine
And turns thy lip to mine,
And mine it is.                                              50

Thou hast a serpent in thine hair,
In all the curls that close and cling;
And ah, thy breast-flower!
Ah love, thy mouth too fair
To kiss and sting!

Cleave to me, love me, kiss mine eyes,
Satiate thy lips with loving me;
Nay, for thou shalt not rise;
Lie still as Love that dies
For love of thee.                                            60

Mine arms are close about thine head,
My lips are fervent on thy face,
And where my kiss hath fed

Thy flower-like blood leaps red
To the kissed place.

O bitterness of things too sweet!
O broken singing of the dove!
Love's wings are over fleet,
And like the panther's feet
The feet of Love. 70

# Satia Te Sanguine

If you loved me ever so little,
   I could bear the bonds that gall,
I could dream the bonds were brittle;
   You do not love me at all.

O beautiful lips, O bosom
   More white than the moon's and warm,
A sterile, a ruinous blossom
   Is blown your way in a storm.

As the lost white feverish limbs
   Of the Lesbian Sappho, adrift
In foam where the sea-weed swims,
   Swam loose for the streams to lift,

My heart swims blind in a sea
   That stuns me; swims to and fro,
And gathers to windward and lee
   Lamentation, and mourning, and woe.

A broken, an emptied boat,
   Sea saps it, winds blow apart,
Sick and adrift and afloat,
   The barren waif of a heart.

Where, when the gods would be cruel,
   Do they go for a torture? where
Plant thorns, set pain like a jewel?
   Ah, not in the flesh, not there!

The racks of earth and the rods
   Are weak as foam on the sands;
In the heart is the prey for gods,
   Who crucify hearts, not hands.

Mere pangs corrode and consume,
   Dead when life dies in the brain;
In the infinite spirit is room
   For the pulse of an infinite pain.

I wish you were dead, my dear;
   I would give you, had I to give,
Some death too bitter to fear;
   It is better to die than live.

I wish you were stricken of thunder
   And burnt with a bright flame through,
Consumed and cloven in sunder,
   I dead at your feet like you.

If I could but know after all,
   I might cease to hunger and ache,
Though your heart were ever so small,
   If it were not a stone or a snake.

You are crueller, you that we love,
   Than hatred, hunger, or death;
You have eyes and breasts like a dove,
   And you kill men's hearts with a breath

As plague in a poisonous city
   Insults and exults on her dead,
So you, when pallid for pity
   Comes love, and fawns to be fed.

As a tame beast writhes and wheedles,
   He fawns to be fed with wiles;
You carve him a cross of needles,
   And whet them sharp as your smiles.

He is patient of thorn and whip,
   He is dumb under axe or dart;
You suck with a sleepy red lip
   The wet red wounds in his heart.

You thrill as his pulses dwindle,
   You brighten and warm as he bleeds,
With insatiable eyes that kindle
   And insatiable mouth that feeds.

Your hands nailed love to the tree,
   You stript him, scourged him with rods,
And drowned him deep in the sea
   That hides the dead and their gods.

And for all this, die will he not;
   There is no man sees him but I;          70
You came and went and forgot;
   I hope he will some day die.

# In the Orchard
(PROVENÇAL BURDEN)

Leave go my hands, let me catch breath and see;
Let the dew-fall drench either side of me;
   Clear apple-leaves are soft upon that moon
Seen sidelong like a blossom in the tree;
   Ah God, ah God, that day should be so soon.

The grass is thick and cool, it lets us lie.
Kissed upon either cheek and either eye,
   I turn to thee as some green afternoon
Turns toward sunset, and is loth to die;
   Ah God, ah God, that day should be so soon.         10

Lie closer, lean your face upon my side,
Feel where the dew fell that has hardly dried,
   Hear how the blood beats that went nigh to swoon;
The pleasure lives there when the sense has died;
   Ah God, ah God, that day should be so soon.

O my fair lord, I charge you leave me this:
Is it not sweeter than a foolish kiss?
   Nay take it then, my flower, my first in June,
My rose, so like a tender mouth it is:
   Ah God, ah God, that day should be so soon.         20

Love, till dawn sunder night from day with fire,
Dividing my delight and my desire,
   The crescent life and love the plenilune,
Love me though dusk begin and dark retire;
   Ah God, ah God, that day should be so soon.

Ah, my heart fails, my blood draws back; I know,
When life runs over, life is near to go;
   And with the slain of love love's ways are strewn,
And with their blood, if love will have it so;
   Ah God, ah God, that day should be so soon.         30

Ah, do thy will now; slay me if thou wilt;
There is no building now the walls are built,
   No quarrying now the corner-stone is hewn,
No drinking now the vine's whole blood is spilt;
   Ah God, ah God, that day should be so soon.

Nay, slay me now; nay, for I will be slain;
Pluck thy red pleasure from the teeth of pain,
   Break down thy vine ere yet grape-gatherers prune,
Slay me ere day can slay desire again;
   Ah God, ah God, that day should be so soon.     40

Yea, with thy sweet lips, with thy sweet sword; yea,
Take life and all, for I will die, I say;
   Love, I gave love, is life a better boon?
For sweet night's sake I will not live till day;
   Ah God, ah God, that day should be so soon.

Nay, I will sleep then only; nay, but go.
Ah sweet, too sweet to me, my sweet, I know
   Love, sleep, and death go to the sweet same tune;
Hold my hair fast, and kiss me through it so.
   Ah God, ah God, that day should be so soon.     50

# A Match

If love were what the rose is,
   And I were like the leaf,
Our lives would grow together
In sad or singing weather,
Blown fields or flowerful closes,
   Green pleasure or grey grief;
If love were what the rose is,
   And I were like the leaf.

If I were what the words are,
   And love were like the tune,
With double sound and single
Delight our lips would mingle,
With kisses glad as birds are
   That get sweet rain at noon;
If I were what the words are,
   And love were like the tune.

If you were life, my darling,
   And I your love were death,
We'd shine and snow together
Ere March made sweet the weather
With daffodil and starling
   And hours of fruitful breath;
If you were life, my darling,
   And I your love were death.

If you were thrall to sorrow,
   And I were page to joy,
We'd play for lives and seasons
With loving looks and treasons
And tears of night and morrow
   And laughs of maid and boy;
If you were thrall to sorrow,
   And I were page to joy.

If you were April's lady,
   And I were lord in May,
We'd throw with leaves for hours
And draw for days with flowers,
Till day like night were shady
   And night were bright like day;
If you were April's lady,
   And I were lord in May.                     40

If you were queen of pleasure,
   And I were king of pain,
We'd hunt down love together,
Pluck out his flying-feather,
And teach his feet a measure,
   And find his mouth a rein;
If you were queen of pleasure,
   And I were king of pain.

# Faustine

*Ave Faustina Imperatrix, morituri te salutant.*

Lean back, and get some minutes' peace;
    Let your head lean
Back to the shoulder with its fleece
    Of locks, Faustine.

The shapely silver shoulder stoops,
    Weighed over clean
With state of splendid hair that droops
    Each side, Faustine.

Let me go over your good gifts
    That crown you queen;
A queen whose kingdom ebbs and shifts
    Each week, Faustine.

Bright heavy brows well gathered up:
    White gloss and sheen;
Carved lips that make my lips a cup
    To drink, Faustine,

Wine and rank poison, milk and blood,
    Being mixed therein
Since first the devil threw dice with God
    For you, Faustine.

Your naked new-born soul, their stake,
    Stood blind between;
God said "let him that wins her take
    And keep Faustine."

But this time Satan throve, no doubt;
    Long since, I ween,
God's part in you was battered out;
    Long since, Faustine.

The die rang sideways as it fell,
    Rang cracked and thin,                                 30
Like a man's laughter heard in hell
    Far down, Faustine,

A shadow of laughter like a sigh,
    Dead sorrow's kin;
So rang, thrown down, the devil's die
    That won Faustine.

A suckling of his breed you were,
    One hard to wean;
But God, who lost you, left you fair,
    We see, Faustine.                                      40

You have the face that suits a woman
    For her soul's screen—
The sort of beauty that's called human
    In hell, Faustine.

You could do all things but be good
    Or chaste of mien;
And that you would not if you could,
    We know, Faustine.

Even he who cast seven devils out
    Of Magdalene                                        50
Could hardly do as much, I doubt,
    For you, Faustine.

Did Satan make you to spite God?
    Or did God mean
To scourge with scorpions for a rod
    Our sins, Faustine?

I know what queen at first you were,
    As though I had seen
Red gold and black imperious hair
    Twice crown Faustine.                           60

As if your fed sarcophagus
    Spared flesh and skin,
You come back face to face with us,
    The same Faustine.

She loved the games men played with death,
    Where death must win;
As though the slain man's blood and breath
    Revived Faustine.

Nets caught the pike, pikes tore the net;
    Lithe limbs and lean                                70
From drained-out pores dripped thick red sweat
    To soothe Faustine.

She drank the steaming drift and dust
    Blown off the scene;
Blood could not ease the bitter lust
    That galled Faustine.

All round the foul fat furrows reeked,
    Where blood sank in;
The circus splashed and seethed and shrieked
    All round Faustine.                                80

But these are gone now: years entomb
    The dust and din;
Yea, even the bath's fierce reek and fume
    That slew Faustine.

Was life worth living then? and now
    Is life worth sin?
Where are the imperial years? and how
    Are you Faustine?

Your soul forgot her joys, forgot
    Her times of teen;                                 90
Yea, this life likewise will you not
    Forget, Faustine?

For in the time we know not of
    Did fate begin
Weaving the web of days that wove
    Your doom, Faustine.

The threads were wet with wine, and all
    Were smooth to spin;
They wove you like a Bacchanal,
    The first Faustine.                                           100

And Bacchus cast your mates and you
    Wild grapes to glean;
Your flower-like lips were dashed with dew
    From his, Faustine.

Your drenched loose hands were stretched to hold
    The vine's wet green,
Long ere they coined in Roman gold
    Your face, Faustine.

Then after change of soaring feather
    And winnowing fin,                                          110
You woke in weeks of feverish weather,
    A new Faustine.

A star upon your birthday burned,
    Whose fierce serene
Red pulseless planet never yearned
    In heaven, Faustine.

Stray breaths of Sapphic song that blew
    Through Mitylene
Shook the fierce quivering blood in you
    By night, Faustine.                                        120

The shameless nameless love that makes
    Hell's iron gin
Shut on you like a trap that breaks
    The soul, Faustine.

And when your veins were void and dead,
    What ghosts unclean
Swarmed round the straitened barren bed
    That hid Faustine?

What sterile growths of sexless root
    Or epicene?
What flower of kisses without fruit
    Of love, Faustine?

What adders came to shed their coats?
    What coiled obscene
Small serpents with soft stretching throats
    Caressed Faustine?

But the time came of famished hours,
    Maimed loves and mean,
This ghastly thin-faced time of ours,
    To spoil Faustine.

You seem a thing that hinges hold,
    A love-machine
With clockwork joints of supple gold—
    No more, Faustine.

Not godless, for you serve one God,
    The Lampsacene,
Who metes the gardens with his rod;
    Your lord, Faustine.

If one should love you with real love
    (Such things have been,
Things your fair face knows nothing of,
    It seems, Faustine);

That clear hair heavily bound back,
    The lights wherein
Shift from dead blue to burnt-up black;
    Your throat, Faustine,

Strong, heavy, throwing out the face
    And hard bright chin
And shameful scornful lips that grace
    Their shame, Faustine,                                    160

Curled lips, long since half kissed away,
    Still sweet and keen;
You'd give him—poison shall we say?
    Or what, Faustine?

# A Cameo

There was a graven image of Desire
    Painted with red blood on a ground of gold
    Passing between the young men and the old,
And by him Pain, whose body shone like fire,
And Pleasure with gaunt hands that grasped their hire.
    Of his left wrist, with fingers clenched and cold,
    The insatiable Satiety kept hold,
Walking with feet unshod that pashed the mire.
The senses and the sorrows and the sins,
    And the strange loves that suck the breasts of Hate     10
Till lips and teeth bite in their sharp indenture,
Followed like beasts with flap of wings and fins.
    Death stood aloof behind a gaping grate,
Upon whose lock was written *Peradventure*.

# The Leper

Nothing is better, I well think,
    Than love; the hidden well-water
    Is not so delicate to drink:
This was well seen of me and her.

I served her in a royal house;
    I served her wine and curious meat.
For will to kiss between her brows,
    I had no heart to sleep or eat.

Mere scorn God knows she had of me,
    A poor scribe, nowise great or fair,     10
Who plucked his clerk's hood back to see
    Her curled-up lips and amorous hair.

I vex my head with thinking this.
    Yea, though God always hated me,
And hates me now that I can kiss
    Her eyes, plait up her hair to see

How she then wore it on the brows,
    Yet am I glad to have her dead
Here in this wretched wattled house
    Where I can kiss her eyes and head.     20

Nothing is better, I well know,
    Than love; no amber in cold sea
Or gathered berries under snow:
    That is well seen of her and me.

Three thoughts I make my pleasure of:
    First I take heart and think of this:
That knight's gold hair she chose to love,
    His mouth she had such will to kiss.

Then I remember that sundawn
    I brought him by a privy way 30
Out at her lattice, and thereon
    What gracious words she found to say.

(Cold rushes for such little feet—
    Both feet could lie into my hand.
A marvel was it of my sweet
    Her upright body could so stand.)

"Sweet friend, God give you thank and grace;
    Now am I clean and whole of shame,
Nor shall men burn me in the face
    For my sweet fault that scandals them." 40

I tell you over word by word.
    She, sitting edgewise on her bed,
Holding her feet, said thus. The third,
    A sweeter thing than these, I said.

God, that makes time and ruins it
    And alters not, abiding God,
Changed with disease her body sweet,
    The body of love wherein she abode.

Love is more sweet and comelier
    Than a dove's throat strained out to sing. 50
All they spat out and cursed at her
    And cast her forth for a base thing.

They cursed her, seeing how God had wrought
    This curse to plague her, a curse of his.
Fools were they surely, seeing not
    How sweeter than all sweet she is.

He that had held her by the hair,
    With kissing lips blinding her eyes,
Felt her bright bosom, strained and bare,
    Sigh under him, with short mad cries 60

Out of her throat and sobbing mouth
   And body broken up with love,
With sweet hot tears his lips were loth
   Her own should taste the savour of,

Yea, he inside whose grasp all night
   Her fervent body leapt or lay,
Stained with sharp kisses red and white,
   Found her a plague to spurn away.

I hid her in this wattled house,
   I served her water and poor bread.               70
For joy to kiss between her brows
   Time upon time I was nigh dead.

Bread failed; we got but well-water
   And gathered grass with dropping seed.
I had such joy of kissing her,
   I had small care to sleep or feed.

Sometimes when service made me glad
   The sharp tears leapt between my lids,
Falling on her, such joy I had
   To do the service God forbids.                80

"I pray you let me be at peace,
   Get hence, make room for me to die."
She said that: her poor lip would cease,
   Put up to mine, and turn to cry.

I said, "Bethink yourself how love
   Fared in us twain, what either did;
Shall I unclothe my soul thereof?
   That I should do this, God forbid."

Yea, though God hateth us, he knows
   That hardly in a little thing                    90
Love faileth of the work it does
   Till it grow ripe for gathering.

Six months, and now my sweet is dead
　　A trouble takes me; I know not
If all were done well, all well said,
　　No word or tender deed forgot.

Too sweet, for the least part in her,
　　To have shed life out by fragments; yet,
Could the close mouth catch breath and stir,
　　I might see something I forget.　　　　　　　　　　100

Six months, and I sit still and hold
　　In two cold palms her cold two feet.
Her hair, half grey half ruined gold,
　　Thrills me and burns me in kissing it.

Love bites and stings me through, to see
　　Her keen face made of sunken bones.
Her worn-off eyelids madden me,
　　That were shot through with purple once.

She said, "Be good with me; I grow
　　So tired for shame's sake, I shall die　　　　　　　110
If you say nothing:" even so.
　　And she is dead now, and shame put by.

Yea, and the scorn she had of me
　　In the old time, doubtless vexed her then.
I never should have kissed her. See
　　What fools God's anger makes of men!

She might have loved me a little too,
　　Had I been humbler for her sake.
But that new shame could make love new
　　She saw not—yet her shame did make.　　　　　　120

I took too much upon my love,
　　Having for such mean service done
Her beauty and all the ways thereof,
　　Her face and all the sweet thereon.

Yea, all this while I tended her,
   I know the old love held fast his part:
I know the old scorn waxed heavier,
   Mixed with sad wonder, in her heart.

It may be all my love went wrong—
   A scribe's work writ awry and blurred,                           130
Scrawled after the blind evensong—
   Spoilt music with no perfect word.

But surely I would fain have done
   All things the best I could. Perchance
Because I failed, came short of one,
   She kept at heart that other man's.

I am grown blind with all these things:
   It may be now she hath in sight
Some better knowledge; still there clings
   The old question. Will not God do right?*                 140

---

\* En ce temps-là estoyt dans ce pays grand nombre de ladres et de meseaulx, ce dont le roy eut grand desplaisir, veu que Dieu dust en estre moult griefvement courroucé. Ores il advint qu'une noble damoyselle appelée Yolande de Sallières estant atteincte et touste guastée de ce vilain mal, tous ses amys et ses parens ayant devant leurs yeux la paour de Dieu la firent issir fors de leurs maisons et oncques ne voulurent recepvoir ni reconforter chose mauldicte de Dieu et à tous les hommes puante et abhominable. Ceste dame avoyt esté moult belle et gracieuse de formes, et de son corps elle estoyt large et de vie lascive. Pourtant nul des amans qui l'avoyent souventesfois accolée et baisée moult tendrement ne voulust plus héberger si laide femme et si détestable pescheresse. Ung seul clerc qui feut premièrement son lacquays et son entremetteur en matière d'amour la reçut chez luy et la récéla dans une petite cabane. Là mourut la meschinette de grande misère et de male mort: et après elle décéda ledist clerc qui pour grand amour l'avoyt six mois durant soignée, lavée, habillée et deshabillée tous les jours de ses mains propres. Mesme dist-on que ce meschant homme et mauldict clerc se remémourant de la grande beauté passée et guastée de ceste femme se délectoyt maintesfois à la baiser sur sa bouche orde et lépreuse et l'accoller doulcement de ses mains amoureuses. Aussy est-il mort de ceste mesme maladie abhominable. Cecy advint près Fontainebellant en Gastinois. Et quand ouyt le roy Philippe ceste adventure moult en estoyt esmerveillé.

                                              *Grandes Chroniques de France*, 1505.

# Erotion

Sweet for a little even to fear, and sweet,
O love, to lay down fear at love's fair feet;
Shall not some fiery memory of his breath
Lie sweet on lips that touch the lips of death?
Yet leave me not; yet, if thou wilt, be free;
Love me no more, but love my love of thee.
Love where thou wilt, and live thy life; and I,
One thing I can, and one love cannot—die.
Pass from me; yet thine arms, thine eyes, thine hair,
Feed my desire and deaden my despair.   10
Yet once more ere time change us, ere my cheek
Whiten, ere hope be dumb or sorrow speak,
Yet once more ere thou hate me, one full kiss;
Keep other hours for others, save me this.
Yea, and I will not (if it please thee) weep,
Lest thou be sad; I will but sigh, and sleep.
Sweet, does death hurt? thou canst not do me wrong:
I shall not lack thee, as I loved thee, long.
Hast thou not given me above all that live
Joy, and a little sorrow shalt not give?   20
What even though fairer fingers of strange girls
Pass nestling through thy beautiful boy's curls
As mine did, or those curled lithe lips of thine
Meet theirs as these, all theirs come after mine;
And though I were not, though I be not, best,
I have loved and love thee more than all the rest.
O love, O lover, loose or hold me fast,
I had thee first, whoever have thee last;
Fairer or not, what need I know, what care?
To thy fair bud my blossom once seemed fair.   30
Why am I fair at all before thee, why
At all desired? seeing thou art fair, not I.
I shall be glad of thee, O fairest head,
Alive, alone, without thee, with thee, dead;
I shall remember while the light lives yet,
And in the night-time I shall not forget.

Though (as thou wilt) thou leave me ere life leave,
I will not, for thy love I will not, grieve;
Not as they use who love not more than I,
Who love not as I love thee though I die;    40
And though thy lips, once mine, be oftener prest
To many another brow and balmier breast,
And sweeter arms, or sweeter to thy mind,
Lull thee or lure, more fond thou wilt not find.

# Before Dawn

Sweet life, if life were stronger,
Earth clear of years that wrong her,
Then two things might live longer,
    Two sweeter things than they;
Delight, the rootless flower,
And love, the bloomless bower;
Delight that lives an hour,
    And love that lives a day.

From evensong to daytime,
When April melts in Maytime,     10
Love lengthens out his playtime,
    Love lessens breath by breath,
And kiss by kiss grows older
On listless throat or shoulder
Turned sideways now, turned colder
    Than life that dreams of death.

This one thing once worth giving
Life gave, and seemed worth living;
Sin sweet beyond forgiving
    And brief beyond regret:     20
To laugh and love together
And weave with foam and feather
And wind and words the tether
    Our memories play with yet.

Ah, one thing worth beginning,
One thread in life worth spinning,
Ah sweet, one sin worth sinning
    With all the whole soul's will;
To lull you till one stilled you,
To kiss you till one killed you,     30
To feed you till one filled you,
    Sweet lips, if love could fill;

To hunt sweet Love and lose him
Between white arms and bosom,
Between the bud and blossom,
   Between your throat and chin;
To say of shame—what is it?
Of virtue—we can miss it,
Of sin—we can but kiss it,
   And it's no longer sin:                        40

To feel the strong soul, stricken
Through fleshly pulses, quicken
Beneath swift sighs that thicken,
   Soft hands and lips that smite;
Lips that no love can tire,
With hands that sting like fire,
Weaving the web Desire
   To snare the bird Delight.

But love so lightly plighted,
Our love with torch unlighted,                      50
Paused near us unaffrighted,
   Who found and left him free;
None, seeing us cloven in sunder,
Will weep or laugh or wonder;
Light love stands clear of thunder,
   And safe from winds at sea.

As, when late larks give warning
Of dying lights and dawning,
Night murmurs to the morning,                    60
   "Lie still, O love, lie still;"
And half her dark limbs cover
The white limbs of her lover,
With amorous plumes that hover
   And fervent lips that chill;

As scornful day represses
Night's void and vain caresses,
And from her cloudier tresses

   Unwinds the gold of his,
With limbs from limbs dividing
And breath by breath subsiding;                                   70
For love has no abiding,
   But dies before the kiss;

So hath it been, so be it;
For who shall live and flee it?
But look that no man see it
   Or hear it unaware;
Lest all who love and choose him
See Love, and so refuse him;
For all who find him lose him,
   But all have found him fair.                                  80

# Dolores
### (NOTRE-DAME DES SEPT DOULEURS)

Cold eyelids that hide like a jewel
  Hard eyes that grow soft for an hour;
The heavy white limbs, and the cruel
  Red mouth like a venomous flower;
When these are gone by with their glories,
  What shall rest of thee then, what remain,
O mystic and sombre Dolores,
  Our Lady of Pain?

Seven sorrows the priests give their Virgin;
  But thy sins, which are seventy times seven,     10
Seven ages would fail thee to purge in,
  And then they would haunt thee in heaven:
Fierce midnights and famishing morrows,
  And the loves that complete and control
All the joys of the flesh, all the sorrows
  That wear out the soul.

O garment not golden but gilded,
  O garden where all men may dwell,
O tower not of ivory, but builded
  By hands that reach heaven from hell;     20
O mystical rose of the mire,
  O house not of gold but of gain,
O house of unquenchable fire,
  Our Lady of Pain!

O lips full of lust and of laughter,
  Curled snakes that are fed from my breast,
Bite hard, lest remembrance come after
  And press with new lips where you pressed.
For my heart too springs up at the pressure,
  Mine eyelids too moisten and burn;     30
Ah, feed me and fill me with pleasure,
  Ere pain come in turn.

In yesterday's reach and to-morrow's,
    Out of sight though they lie of to-day,
There have been and there yet shall be sorrows
    That smite not and bite not in play.
The life and the love thou despisest,
    These hurt us indeed, and in vain,
O wise among women, and wisest,
    Our Lady of Pain.    40

Who gave thee thy wisdom? what stories
    That stung thee, what visions that smote?
Wert thou pure and a maiden, Dolores,
    When desire took thee first by the throat?
What bud was the shell of a blossom
    That all men may smell to and pluck?
What milk fed thee first at what bosom?
    What sins gave thee suck?

We shift and bedeck and bedrape us,
    Thou art noble and nude and antique;    50
Libitina thy mother, Priapus
    Thy father, a Tuscan and Greek.
We play with light loves in the portal,
    And wince and relent and refrain;
Loves die, and we know thee immortal,
    Our Lady of Pain.

Fruits fail and love dies and time ranges;
    Thou art fed with perpetual breath,
And alive after infinite changes,
    And fresh from the kisses of death;    60
Of languors rekindled and rallied,
    Of barren delights and unclean,
Things monstrous and fruitless, a pallid
    And poisonous queen.

Could you hurt me, sweet lips, though I hurt you?
    Men touch them, and change in a trice
The lilies and languors of virtue

For the raptures and roses of vice;
Those lie where thy foot on the floor is,
   These crown and caress thee and chain,
O splendid and sterile Dolores,
   Our Lady of Pain.

There are sins it may be to discover,
   There are deeds it may be to delight.
What new work wilt thou find for thy lover,
   What new passions for daytime or night?
What spells that they know not a word of
   Whose lives are as leaves overblown?
What tortures undreamt of, unheard of,
   Unwritten, unknown?

Ah beautiful passionate body
   That never has ached with a heart!
On thy mouth though the kisses are bloody,
   Though they sting till it shudder and smart,
More kind than the love we adore is,
   They hurt not the heart or the brain,
O bitter and tender Dolores,
   Our Lady of Pain.

As our kisses relax and redouble,
   From the lips and the foam and the fangs
Shall no new sin be born for men's trouble,
   No dream of impossible pangs?
With the sweet of the sins of old ages
   Wilt thou satiate thy soul as of yore?
Too sweet is the rind, say the sages,
   Too bitter the core.

Hast thou told all thy secrets the last time,
   And bared all thy beauties to one?
Ah, where shall we go then for pastime,
   If the worst that can be has been done?
But sweet as the rind was the core is;
   We are fain of thee still, we are fain,
O sanguine and subtle Dolores,
   Our Lady of Pain.

By the hunger of change and emotion,
    By the thirst of unbearable things,
By despair, the twin-born of devotion,
    By the pleasure that winces and stings,
The delight that consumes the desire,
    The desire that outruns the delight,            110
By the cruelty deaf as a fire
    And blind as the night,

By the ravenous teeth that have smitten
    Through the kisses that blossom and bud,
By the lips intertwisted and bitten
    Till the foam has a savour of blood,
By the pulse as it rises and falters,
    By the hands as they slacken and strain,
I adjure thee, respond from thine altars,
    Our Lady of Pain.            120

Wilt thou smile as a woman disdaining
    The light fire in the veins of a boy?
But he comes to thee sad, without feigning,
    Who has wearied of sorrow and joy;
Less careful of labour and glory
    Than the elders whose hair has uncurled:
And young, but with fancies as hoary
    And grey as the world.

I have passed from the outermost portal
    To the shrine where a sin is a prayer;        130
What care though the service be mortal?
    O our Lady of Torture, what care?
All thine the last wine that I pour is,
    The last in the chalice we drain,
O fierce and luxurious Dolores,
    Our Lady of Pain.

All thine the new wine of desire,
    The fruit of four lips as they clung
Till the hair and the eyelids took fire,
    The foam of a serpentine tongue,        140

The froth of the serpents of pleasure,
    More salt than the foam of the sea,
Now felt as a flame, now at leisure
    As wine shed for me.

Ah thy people, thy children, thy chosen,
    Marked cross from the womb and perverse!
They have found out the secret to cozen
    The gods that constrain us and curse;
They alone, they are wise, and none other;
    Give me place, even me, in their train,           150
O my sister, my spouse, and my mother,
    Our Lady of Pain.

For the crown of our life as it closes
    Is darkness, the fruit thereof dust;
No thorns go as deep as a rose's,
    And love is more cruel than lust.
Time turns the old days to derision,
    Our loves into corpses or wives;
And marriage and death and division
    Make barren our lives.           160

And pale from the past we draw nigh thee,
    And satiate with comfortless hours;
And we know thee, how all men belie thee,
    And we gather the fruit of thy flowers;
The passion that slays and recovers,
    The pangs and the kisses that rain
On the lips and the limbs of thy lovers,
    Our Lady of Pain.

The desire of thy furious embraces
    Is more than the wisdom of years,           170
On the blossom though blood lie in traces,
    Though the foliage be sodden with tears.
For the lords in whose keeping the door is
    That opens on all who draw breath
Gave the cypress to love, my Dolores,
    The myrtle to death.

And they laughed, changing hands in the measure,
   And they mixed and made peace after strife;
Pain melted in tears, and was pleasure;
   Death tingled with blood, and was life.
Like lovers they melted and tingled,
   In the dusk of thine innermost fane;
In the darkness they murmured and mingled,
   Our Lady of Pain.

In a twilight where virtues are vices,
   In thy chapels, unknown of the sun,
To a tune that enthralls and entices,
   They were wed, and the twain were as one.
For the tune from thine altar hath sounded
   Since God bade the world's work begin,
And the fume of thine incense abounded,
   To sweeten the sin.

Love listens, and paler than ashes,
   Through his curls as the crown on them slips,
Lifts languid wet eyelids and lashes,
   And laughs with insatiable lips.
Thou shalt hush him with heavy caresses,
   With music that scares the profane;
Thou shalt darken his eyes with thy tresses,
   Our Lady of Pain.

Thou shalt blind his bright eyes though he wrestle,
   Thou shalt chain his light limbs though he strive;
In his lips all thy serpents shall nestle,
   In his hands all thy cruelties thrive.
In the daytime thy voice shall go through him,
   In his dreams he shall feel thee and ache;
Thou shalt kindle by night and subdue him
   Asleep and awake.

Thou shalt touch and make redder his roses
   With juice not of fruit nor of bud;
When the sense in the spirit reposes,
   Thou shalt quicken the soul through the blood.

Thine, thine the one grace we implore is,
   Who would live and not languish or feign,
O sleepless and deadly Dolores,
   Our Lady of Pain.

Dost thou dream, in a respite of slumber,
   In a lull of the fires of thy life,
Of the days without name, without number,
   When thy will stung the world into strife;                220
When, a goddess, the pulse of thy passion
   Smote kings as they revelled in Rome;
And they hailed thee re-risen, O Thalassian,
   Foam-white, from the foam?

When thy lips had such lovers to flatter;
   When the city lay red from thy rods,
And thine hands were as arrows to scatter
   The children of change and their gods;
When the blood of thy foemen made fervent
   A sand never moist from the main,                        230
As one smote them, their lord and thy servant,
   Our Lady of Pain.

On sands by the storm never shaken,
   Nor wet from the washing of tides;
Nor by foam of the waves overtaken,
   Nor winds that the thunder bestrides;
But red from the print of thy paces,
   Made smooth for the world and its lords,
Ringed round with a flame of fair faces,
   And splendid with swords.                                240

There the gladiator, pale for thy pleasure,
   Drew bitter and perilous breath;
There torments laid hold on the treasure
   Of limbs too delicious for death;
When thy gardens were lit with live torches;
   When the world was a steed for thy rein;
When the nations lay prone in thy porches,
   Our Lady of Pain.

When, with flame all around him aspirant,
    Stood flushed, as a harp-player stands,    250
The implacable beautiful tyrant,
    Rose-crowned, having death in his hands;
And a sound as the sound of loud water
    Smote far through the flight of the fires,
And mixed with the lightning of slaughter
    A thunder of lyres.

Dost thou dream of what was and no more is,
    The old kingdoms of earth and the kings?
Dost thou hunger for these things, Dolores,
    For these, in a world of new things?    260
But thy bosom no fasts could emaciate,
    No hunger compel to complain
Those lips that no bloodshed could satiate,
    Our Lady of Pain.

As of old when the world's heart was lighter,
    Through thy garments the grace of thee glows,
The white wealth of thy body made whiter
    By the blushes of amorous blows,
And seamed with sharp lips and fierce fingers,
    And branded by kisses that bruise;    270
When all shall be gone that now lingers,
    Ah, what shall we lose?

Thou wert fair in the fearless old fashion,
    And thy limbs are as melodies yet,
And move to the music of passion
    With lithe and lascivious regret.
What ailed us, O gods, to desert you
    For creeds that refuse and restrain?
Come down and redeem us from virtue,
    Our Lady of Pain.    280

All shrines that were Vestal are flameless,
    But the flame has not fallen from this;
Though obscure be the god, and though nameless
    The eyes and the hair that we kiss;

Low fires that love sits by and forges
    Fresh heads for his arrows and thine;
Hair loosened and soiled in mid orgies
    With kisses and wine.

Thy skin changes country and colour,
    And shrivels or swells to a snake's.            290
Let it brighten and bloat and grow duller,
    We know it, the flames and the flakes,
Red brands on it smitten and bitten,
    Round skies where a star is a stain,
And the leaves with thy litanies written,
    Our Lady of Pain.

On thy bosom though many a kiss be,
    There are none such as knew it of old.
Was it Alciphron once or Arisbe,
    Male ringlets or feminine gold,              300
That thy lips met with under the statue,
    Whence a look shot out sharp after thieves
From the eyes of the garden-god at you
    Across the fig-leaves?

Then still, through dry seasons and moister,
    One god had a wreath to his shrine;
Then love was the pearl of his oyster,[1]
    And Venus rose red out of wine.
We have all done amiss, choosing rather
    Such loves as the wise gods disdain;          310
Intercede for us thou with thy father,
    Our Lady of Pain.

In spring he had crowns of his garden,
    Red corn in the heat of the year,
Then hoary green olives that harden
    When the grape-blossom freezes with fear;
And milk-budded myrtles with Venus

---

[1] Nam te præcipuè in suis urbibus colit ora
    Hellespontia, cæteris ostreosior oris.
                        CATULL. *Carm.* xviii.

And vine-leaves with Bacchus he trod;
And ye said, "We have seen, he hath seen us,
   A visible God."                                                     320

What broke off the garlands that girt you?
   What sundered you spirit and clay?
Weak sins yet alive are as virtue
   To the strength of the sins of that day.
For dried is the blood of thy lover,
   Ipsithilla, contracted the vein;
Cry aloud, "Will he rise and recover,
   Our Lady of Pain?"

Cry aloud; for the old world is broken:
   Cry out; for the Phrygian is priest,                  330
And rears not the bountiful token
   And spreads not the fatherly feast.
From the midmost of Ida, from shady
   Recesses that murmur at morn,
They have brought and baptized her, Our Lady,
   A goddess new-born.

And the chaplets of old are above us,
   And the oyster-bed teems out of reach;
Old poets outsing and outlove us,
   And Catullus makes mouths at our speech.       340
Who shall kiss, in thy father's own city,
   With such lips as he sang with, again?
Intercede for us all of thy pity,
   Our Lady of Pain.

Out of Dindymus heavily laden
   Her lions draw bound and unfed
A mother, a mortal, a maiden,
   A queen over death and the dead.
She is cold, and her habit is lowly,
   Her temple of branches and sods;                    350
Most fruitful and virginal, holy,
   A mother of gods.

She hath wasted with fire thine high places,
    She hath hidden and marred and made sad
The fair limbs of the Loves, the fair faces
    Of gods that were goodly and glad.
She slays, and her hands are not bloody;
    She moves as a moon in the wane,
White-robed, and thy raiment is ruddy,
    Our Lady of Pain.                                                360

They shall pass and their places be taken,
    The gods and the priests that are pure.
They shall pass, and shalt thou not be shaken?
    They shall perish, and shalt thou endure?
Death laughs, breathing close and relentless
    In the nostrils and eyelids of lust,
With a pinch in his fingers of scentless
    And delicate dust.

But the worm shall revive thee with kisses;
    Thou shalt change and transmute as a god,              370
As the rod to a serpent that hisses,
    As the serpent again to a rod.
Thy life shall not cease though thou doff it;
    Thou shalt live until evil be slain,
And good shall die first, said thy prophet,
    Our Lady of Pain.

Did he lie? did he laugh? does he know it,
    Now he lies out of reach, out of breath,
Thy prophet, thy preacher, thy poet,
    Sin's child by incestuous Death?                                380
Did he find out in fire at his waking,
    Or discern as his eyelids lost light,
When the bands of the body were breaking
    And all came in sight?

Who has known all the evil before us,
    Or the tyrannous secrets of time?
Though we match not the dead men that bore us
    At a song, at a kiss, at a crime—

Though the heathen outface and outlive us,
    And our lives and our longings are twain—
Ah, forgive us our virtues, forgive us,
    Our Lady of Pain.

Who are we that embalm and embrace thee
    With spices and savours of song?
What is time, that his children should face thee?
    What am I, that my lips do thee wrong?
I could hurt thee—but pain would delight thee;
    Or caress thee—but love would repel;
And the lovers whose lips would excite thee
    Are serpents in hell.

Who now shall content thee as they did,
    Thy lovers, when temples were built
And the hair of the sacrifice braided
    And the blood of the sacrifice spilt,
In Lampsacus fervent with faces,
    In Aphaca red from thy reign,
Who embraced thee with awful embraces,
    Our Lady of Pain?

Where are they, Cotytto or Venus,
    Astarte or Ashtaroth, where?
Do their hands as we touch come between us?
    Is the breath of them hot in thy hair?
From their lips have thy lips taken fever,
    With the blood of their bodies grown red?
Hast thou left upon earth a believer
    If these men are dead?

They were purple of raiment and golden,
    Filled full of thee, fiery with wine,
Thy lovers, in haunts unbeholden,
    In marvellous chambers of thine.
They are fled, and their footprints escape us,
    Who appraise thee, adore, and abstain,
O daughter of Death and Priapus,
    Our Lady of Pain.

What ails us to fear overmeasure,
   To praise thee with timorous breath,
O mistress and mother of pleasure,
   The one thing as certain as death?
We shall change as the things that we cherish,
   Shall fade as they faded before,                                         430
As foam upon water shall perish,
   As sand upon shore.

We shall know what the darkness discovers,
   If the grave-pit be shallow or deep;
And our fathers of old, and our lovers,
   We shall know if they sleep not or sleep.
We shall see whether hell be not heaven,
   Find out whether tares be not grain,
And the joys of thee seventy times seven,
   Our Lady of Pain.                                                            440

# Sapphics

All the night sleep came not upon my eyelids,
Shed not dew, nor shook nor unclosed a feather,
Yet with lips shut close and with eyes of iron
    Stood and beheld me.

Then to me so lying awake a vision
Came without sleep over the seas and touched me,
Softly touched mine eyelids and lips; and I too,
    Full of the vision,

Saw the white implacable Aphrodite,
Saw the hair unbound and the feet unsandalled        10
Shine as fire of sunset on western waters;
    Saw the reluctant

Feet, the straining plumes of the doves that drew her,
Looking always, looking with necks reverted,
Back to Lesbos, back to the hills whereunder
    Shone Mitylene;

Heard the flying feet of the Loves behind her
Make a sudden thunder upon the waters,
As the thunder flung from the strong unclosing
    Wings of a great wind.        20

So the goddess fled from her place, with awful
Sound of feet and thunder of wings around her;
While behind a clamour of singing women
    Severed the twilight.

Ah the singing, ah the delight, the passion!
All the Loves wept, listening; sick with anguish,
Stood the crowned nine Muses about Apollo;
    Fear was upon them,

While the tenth sang wonderful things they knew not.
Ah the tenth, the Lesbian! the nine were silent, 30
None endured the sound of her song for weeping;
    Laurel by laurel,

Faded all their crowns; but about her forehead,
Round her woven tresses and ashen temples
White as dead snow, paler than grass in summer,
    Ravaged with kisses,

Shone a light of fire as a crown for ever.
Yea, almost the implacable Aphrodite
Paused, and almost wept; such a song was that song.
    Yea, by her name too 40

Called her, saying, "Turn to me, O my Sappho;"
Yet she turned her face from the Loves, she saw not
Tears for laughter darken immortal eyelids,
    Heard not about her

Fearful fitful wings of the doves departing,
Saw not how the bosom of Aphrodite
Shook with weeping, saw not her shaken raiment,
    Saw not her hands wrung;

Saw the Lesbians kissing across their smitten
Lutes with lips more sweet than the sound of lute-strings, 50
Mouth to mouth and hand upon hand, her chosen,
    Fairer than all men;

Only saw the beautiful lips and fingers,
Full of songs and kisses and little whispers,
Full of music; only beheld among them
    Soar, as a bird soars

Newly fledged, her visible song, a marvel,
Made of perfect sound and exceeding passion,
Sweetly shapen, terrible, full of thunders,
    Clothed with the wind's wings. 60

Then rejoiced she, laughing with love, and scattered
Roses, awful roses of holy blossom;
Then the Loves thronged sadly with hidden faces
    Round Aphrodite,

Then the Muses, stricken at heart, were silent;
Yea, the gods waxed pale; such a song was that song.
All reluctant, all with a fresh repulsion,
    Fled from before her.

All withdrew long since, and the land was barren,
Full of fruitless women and music only.     70
Now perchance, when winds are assuaged at sunset,
    Lulled at the dewfall,

By the grey sea-side, unassuaged, unheard of,
Unbeloved, unseen in the ebb of twilight,
Ghosts of outcast women return lamenting,
    Purged not in Lethe,

Clothed about with flame and with tears, and singing
Songs that move the heart of the shaken heaven,
Songs that break the heart of the earth with pity,
    Hearing, to hear them.     80

# *from* The Masque of Queen Bersabe
### A MIRACLE-PLAY

    HERODIAS
I am the queen Herodias.      132
This headband of my temples was
    King Herod's gold band woven me.
This broken dry staff in my hand
Was the queen's staff of a great land
    Betwixen Perse and Samarie.
For that one dancing of my feet,
The fire is come in my green wheat,
    From one sea to the other sea.     140

    AHOLIBAH
I am the queen Aholibah.
My lips kissed dumb the word of *Ah*
    Sighed on strange lips grown sick thereby.
God wrought to me my royal bed;
The inner work thereof was red,
    The outer work was ivory.
My mouth's heat was the heat of flame
For lust towards the kings that came
    With horsemen riding royally.

    CLEOPATRA
I am the queen of Ethiope.     150
Love bade my kissing eyelids ope
    That men beholding might praise love.
My hair was wonderful and curled;
My lips held fast the mouth o' the world
    To spoil the strength and speech thereof.
The latter triumph in my breath
Bowed down the beaten brows of death,
    Ashamed they had not wrath enough.

    ABIHAIL
I am the queen of Tyrians.

My hair was glorious for twelve spans,          160
    That dried to loose dust afterward.
My stature was a strong man's length:
My neck was like a place of strength
    Built with white walls, even and hard.
Like the first noise of rain leaves catch
One from another, snatch by snatch,
    Is my praise, hissed against and marred.

    AZUBAH
I am the queen of Amorites.
My face was like a place of lights
    With multitudes at festival.          170
The glory of my gracious brows
Was like God's house made glorious
    With colours upon either wall.
Between my brows and hair there was
A white space like a space of glass
    With golden candles over all.

    AHOLAH
I am the queen of Amalek.
There was no tender touch or fleck
    To spoil my body or bared feet.
My words were soft like dulcimers,          180
And the first sweet of grape-flowers
    Made each side of my bosom sweet.
My raiment was as tender fruit
Whose rind smells sweet of spice-tree root,
    Bruised balm-blossom and budded wheat.

    AHINOAM
I am the queen Ahinoam.
Like the throat of a soft slain lamb
    Was my throat, softer veined than his:
My lips were as two grapes the sun
Lays his whole weight of heat upon          190
    Like a mouth heavy with a kiss:
My hair's pure purple a wrought fleece,

My temples therein as a piece
   Of a pomegranate's cleaving is.

   ATARAH
I am the queen Sidonian.
My face made faint the face of man,
   And strength was bound between my brows.
Spikenard was hidden in my ships,
Honey and wheat and myrrh in strips,
   White wools that shine as colour does,                 200
Soft linen dyed upon the fold,
Split spice and cores of scented gold,
   Cedar and broken calamus.

   SEMIRAMIS
I am the queen Semiramis.
The whole world and the sea that is
   In fashion like a chrysopras,
The noise of all men labouring,
The priest's mouth tired through thanksgiving,
   The sound of love in the blood's pause,
The strength of love in the blood's beat,                 210
All these were cast beneath my feet
   And all found lesser than I was.

   HESIONE
I am the queen Hesione.
The seasons that increased in me
   Made my face fairer than all men's.
I had the summer in my hair;
And all the pale gold autumn air
   Was as the habit of my sense.
My body was as fire that shone;
God's beauty that makes all things one                 220
   Was one among my handmaidens.

   CHRYSOTHEMIS
I am the queen of Samothrace.
God, making roses, made my face

As a rose filled up full with red.
My prows made sharp the straitened seas
From Pontus to that Chersonese
    Whereon the ebbed Asian stream is shed.
My hair was as sweet scent that drips;
Love's breath begun about my lips
    Kindled the lips of people dead.

    THOMYRIS
I am the queen of Scythians.
My strength was like no strength of man's,
    My face like day, my breast like spring.
My fame was felt in the extreme land
That hath sunshine on the one hand
    And on the other star-shining.
Yea, and the wind there fails of breath;
Yea, and there life is waste like death;
    Yea, and there death is a glad thing.

    HARHAS
I am the queen of Anakim.
In the spent years whose speech is dim,
    Whose raiment is the dust and death,
My stately body without stain
Shone as the shining race of rain
    Whose hair a great wind scattereth.
Now hath God turned my lips to sighs,
Plucked off mine eyelids from mine eyes,
    And sealed with seals my way of breath.

    MYRRHA
I am the queen Arabian.
The tears wherewith mine eyelids ran
    Smelt like my perfumed eyelids' smell.
A harsh thirst made my soft mouth hard,
That ached with kisses afterward;
    My brain rang like a beaten bell.
As tears on eyes, as fire on wood,
Sin fed upon my breath and blood,
    Sin made my breasts subside and swell.

### PASIPHAE

I am the queen Pasiphae.
Not all the pure clean-coloured sea
   Could cleanse or cool my yearning veins;         260
Nor any root nor herb that grew,
Flag-leaves that let green water through,
   Nor washing of the dews and rains.
From shame's pressed core I wrung the sweet
Fruit's savour that was death to eat,
   Whereof no seed but death remains.

### SAPPHO

I am the queen of Lesbians.
My love, that had no part in man's,
   Was sweeter than all shape of sweet.
The intolerable infinite desire         270
Made my face pale like faded fire
   When the ashen pyre falls through with heat.
My blood was hot wan wine of love,
And my song's sound the sound thereof,
   The sound of the delight of it.

### MESSALINA

I am the queen of Italy.
These were the signs God set on me;
   A barren beauty subtle and sleek,
Curled carven hair, and cheeks worn wan
With fierce false lips of many a man,         280
   Large temples where the blood ran weak,
A mouth athirst and amorous
And hungering as the grave's mouth does
   That, being an-hungred, cannot speak.

### AMESTRIS

I am the queen of Persians.
My breasts were lordlier than bright swans,
   My body as amber fair and thin.
Strange flesh was given my lips for bread,
With poisonous hours my days were fed,

And my feet shod with adder-skin.
In Shushan toward Ecbatane
I wrought my joys with tears and pain,
    My loves with blood and bitter sin.

EPHRATH

I am the queen of Rephaim.
God, that some while refraineth him,
    Made in the end a spoil of me.
My rumour was upon the world
As strong sound of swoln water hurled
    Through porches of the straining sea.
My hair was like the flag-flower,
And my breasts carven goodlier
    Than beryl with chalcedony.

PASITHEA

I am the queen of Cypriotes.
Mine oarsmen, labouring with brown throats,
    Sang of me many a tender thing.
My maidens, girdled loose and braced
With gold from bosom to white waist,
    Praised me between their wool-combing.
All that praise Venus all night long
With lips like speech and lids like song
    Praised me till song lost heart to sing.

ALACIEL

I am the queen Alaciel.
My mouth was like that moist gold cell
    Whereout the thickest honey drips.
Mine eyes were as a grey-green sea;
The amorous blood that smote on me
    Smote to my feet and finger-tips.
My throat was whiter than the dove,
Mine eyelids as the seals of love,
    And as the doors of love my lips.

### ERIGONE

I am the queen Erigone.
The wild wine shed as blood on me
   Made my face brighter than a bride's.
My large lips had the old thirst of earth,
Mine arms the might of the old sea's girth
   Bound round the whole world's iron sides.
Within mine eyes and in mine ears
Were music and the wine of tears,
   And light, and thunder of the tides.

## Love and Sleep

Lying asleep between the strokes of night
   I saw my love lean over my sad bed,
   Pale as the duskiest lily's leaf or head,
Smooth-skinned and dark, with bare throat made to bite,
Too wan for blushing and too warm for white,
   But perfect-coloured without white or red.
   And her lips opened amorously, and said—
I wist not what, saving one word—Delight.
And all her face was honey to my mouth,
   And all her body pasture to mine eyes;
     The long lithe arms and hotter hands than fire,
The quivering flanks, hair smelling of the south,
   The bright light feet, the splendid supple thighs
     And glittering eyelids of my soul's desire.

# Cleopatra

"Her beauty might outface the jealous hours,
Turn shame to love and pain to a tender sleep,
And the strong nerve of hate to sloth and tears;
Make spring rebellious in the sides of frost,
Thrust out lank water with hot August growths,
Compel sweet blood into the husks of death,
And from strange beasts enforce harsh courtesy."
    T. Hayman, *Fall of Antony*, 1655.

I
Her mouth is fragrant as a vine,
 A vine with birds in all its boughs;
Serpent and scarab for a sign
 Between the beauty of her brows
And the amorous deep lids divine.

II
Her great curled hair makes luminous
 Her cheeks, her lifted throat and chin.
Shall she not have the hearts of us
 To shatter, and the loves therein
To shred between her fingers thus?       10

III
Small ruined broken strays of light,
 Pearl after pearl she shreds them through
Her long sweet sleepy fingers, white
 As any pearl's heart veined with blue,
And soft as dew on a soft night.

IV
As if the very eyes of love
 Shone through her shutting lids, and stole
The slow looks of a snake or dove;
 As if her lips absorbed the whole
Of love, her soul the soul thereof.       20

V
Lost, all the lordly pearls that were
    Wrung from the sea's heart, from the green
Coasts of the Indian gulf-river;
    Lost, all the loves of the world—so keen
Towards this queen for love of her.

VI
You see against her throat the small
    Sharp glittering shadows of them shake;
And through her hair the imperial
    Curled likeness of the river snake,
Whose bite shall make an end of all.                          30

VII
Through the scales sheathing him like wings,
    Through hieroglyphs of gold and gem,
The strong sense of her beauty stings,
    Like a keen pulse of love in them,
A running flame through all his rings.

VIII
Under those low large lids of hers
    She hath the histories of all time;
The fruit of foliage-stricken years;
    The old seasons with their heavy chime
That leaves its rhyme in the world's ears.                    40

IX
She sees the hand of death made bare,
    The ravelled riddle of the skies,
The faces faded that were fair,
    The mouths made speechless that were wise,
The hollow eyes and dusty hair;

X
The shape and shadow of mystic things,
    Things that fate fashions or forbids;
The staff of time-forgotten Kings

Whose name falls off the Pyramids,
Their coffin-lids and grave-clothings;

XI
Dank dregs, the scum of pool or clod,
    God-spawn of lizard-footed clans,
And those dog-headed hulks that trod
    Swart necks of the old Egyptians,
Raw draughts of man's beginning God;

XII
The poised hawk, quivering ere he smote,
    With plume-like gems on breast and back;
The asps and water-worms afloat
    Between the rush-flowers moist and slack;
The cat's warm black bright rising throat.

XIII
The purple days of drouth expand
    Like a scroll opened out again;
The molten heaven drier than sand,
    The hot red heaven without rain,
Sheds iron pain on the empty land.

XIV
All Egypt aches in the sun's sight;
    The lips of men are harsh for drouth,
The fierce air leaves their cheeks burnt white,
    Charred by the bitter blowing south,
Whose dusty mouth is sharp to bite.

XV
All this she dreams of, and her eyes
    Are wrought after the sense hereof.
There is no heart in her for sighs;
    The face of her is more than love—
A name above the Ptolemies.

XVI
Her great grave beauty covers her
  As that sleek spoil beneath her feet
Clothed once the anointed soothsayer;
  The hallowing is gone forth from it
Now, made unmeet for priests to wear.                              80

XVII
She treads on gods and god-like things,
  On fate and fear and life and death,
On hate that cleaves and love that clings,
  All that is brought forth of man's breath
And perisheth with what it brings.

XVIII
She holds her future close, her lips
  Hold fast the face of things to be;
Actium, and sound of war that dips
  Down the blown valleys of the sea,
Far sails that flee, and storms of ships;                          90

XIX
The laughing red sweet mouth of wine
  At ending of life's festival;
That spice of cerecloths, and the fine
  White bitter dust funereal
Sprinkled on all things for a sign;

XX
His face, who was and was not he,
  In whom, alive, her life abode;
The end, when she gained heart to see
  Those ways of death wherein she trod,
Goddess by god, with Antony.                                       100

## from Pasiphae [a dramatic fragment]

DAEDALUS
O might of man & marvellous handicraft,
What great work have ye done, serving the soul,
Both here & in all places of all time,
Now chiefliest serving, now this goodly shape
Stands excellent, a cunning carven beast,
Made to my mind out of well-laboured wood,
Fit for a fair queen's body to creep in
And hide & suck the liberal juice of joy
Drinking with mere beast's mouth a god's delight!
For with the strong drink of salt-tasted love           10
Shall her desire be saturated & feed
Till it wax faint & glut the belly & womb
At all obscure & delicate orifices,
And at all pores of permeated flesh
Soak itself to the soul with honey-seed,
Sweet stings & pleasurable warm violences
And shoots of fluid flame through the aching blood
And drench of draughts not drunken at the mouth.
This say I now by queen Pasiphae,
As whom the sharp goad of an amorous will               20
Pricks to the bone, biting her flesh with teeth
Immedicable, a wider-waxing wound.
Nor on her dreamless eyelids does the night
Sit peaceable, nor day with staff of gold
Beat off the violent thoughts that vex her brain.
For when man's heart is hunted of such hounds,
Not with oil rubbed nor any balsam grown
Shall it be salved from seizure of their fangs.
But this I bid gods look to; since on earth
There springs no herb for hurts remediable              30
That can shut up such lips of such a wound.
And now with veiled head & august array,
Queenlike she comes forth to the gold-eyed morn.
Hail thou, the lady of this our land, & be
Happy, so be it God gives thee happiness.

> PASIPHAE
> Hail thou too, the most subtle hand of men,
> Elect of gods for elegance of craft,
> And thankworthy; what hap or hope is ours?

> DAEDALUS
> O queen, good hope is waxen to good hap,
> And of fair blossom fruit is fairer born;                40
> Look if I bid these duly cheer or no.

> PASIPHAE
> O gods, what birth is this then of thy wit?

> DAEDALUS
> Nay, with bare hands was this thing procreated.

> PASIPHAE
> A goodly birth & generative of good.

> DAEDALUS
> So may my spiritual seed bear fleshly fruit—

> PASIPHAE
> As of what graft incorporate with what stem?

> DAEDALUS
> To thy glad body & womb impregnated.

> PASIPHAE
> Thou shewest no shew perspicuous to my sight.

> DAEDALUS
> Set thy face here & say what shew of shape—

> PASIPHAE
> I seem then blind or slant of sight in thine?        50

> DAEDALUS
> Thine eyes drink down beholding what is wrought.

PASIPHAE
Surely the clean shape of a carven cow—

DAEDALUS
So much thou seest, & this with bodily eyes?

PASIPHAE
Hollowed inside & jointed with fit limbs—

DAEDALUS
So thy tongue fitly now sets fit word to word.

PASIPHAE
And fitted with a fell of heavy hair.

DAEDALUS
Seems this to thee then no small subtlety—

PASIPHAE
But rather a feat of some divine device.

DAEDALUS
To have wrought in wood such likeness of a life?

PASIPHAE
Some god then blew breath in between the lips.   60

DAEDALUS
Know that thou seest no god who seest but me.

PASIPHAE
Man, but the gods then over-gave of gifts—

DAEDALUS
Keep thy tongue wary & choose innocuous words—

PASIPHAE
Giving thee thus much more than many men.

##### DAEDALUS
Lest thine eyes weep for thy mouth's hardihood.

##### PASIPHAE
O happiest head, O my life's help & stay,
Be prosperous, & have praise of men & me
In all time alway; but this one thing more,
This will I ask thee, & spare not thou to say,
In what way having put this strange shape on,        70
I may fare heifer-wise beneath a bull,
Being clothed with cow & quite dis-womanized.

##### DAEDALUS
And seasonable in sooth this speech of thine
Seems to me spoken, & not improvident,
Woman; for where good counsel dwells with kings
Under one roof & on one seat enthroned
Wears one crown with them, there the land fares well,
But with kings evil-counselled fares to death.
Thus then in brief shalt thou reap all thy will—

##### PASIPHAE
Blessed of God be thou who has made me so.        80

##### DAEDALUS
Here where this hinge turns inward half the flank—

##### PASIPHAE
O happy doorway to the windening womb.

##### DAEDALUS
Creep thou close in, hiding thy furtive foot—

##### PASIPHAE
By covered ways the warm walled garden through.

##### DAEDALUS
And fitting to the measure of the make—

PASIPHAE
Ah blessed body & bed too sweet for sleep.

DAEDALUS
Thy fair-limbed length & breadth proportionate—

PASIPHAE
Even to the likeness of a four-foot life.

DAEDALUS
Set mouth to mouth, & flesh to wood & take—

PASIPHAE
A sweet thing taken in as sweet a snare.                    90

DAEDALUS
That prey thy soul hunts after without hounds.

PASIPHAE
No spoil for my spear, but a spear for me.

DAEDALUS
And hidden in a thicket of curled hair—

PASIPHAE
Grass leafy-locked of a well-wooded field.

DAEDALUS
Catch thou no fearful fawn nor fugitive—

PASIPHAE
Nor happed with hands or any net staked in—

DAEDALUS
Hard by the foliage-hidden fountain-head—

PASIPHAE
But with glad wrestle & strong long sport o' the spear.

DAEDALUS
That washed in warmer wells than where men drink—

PASIPHAE
Such as the beast that sips of grows to god.                100

DAEDALUS
Thou mayst wax glad & glorious of thy womb.

PASIPHAE
Being wounded with one weapon & made whole.

DAEDALUS
Wounded thou sayest, but woundless is thy thought.

PASIPHAE
My thought says healing while my tongue says hurt.

DAEDALUS
Fare as thou wilt then well in deem & deed.

PASIPHAE
Fare thou too Godward all thy life long well,
Who hast holpen me past hope of help to hope.

DAEDALUS
The rest I known not, but give only God
Grace if there be grace in my hands' work here.

# The Complaint of the Fair Armouress
[*from* Translations from the French of Villon]

I
Meseemeth I heard cry and groan
   That sweet who was the armourer's maid;
For her young years she made sore moan,
   And right upon this wise she said;
   "Ah fierce old age with foul bald head,
To spoil fair things thou art over fain;
   Who holdeth me? who? would God I were dead!
Would God I were well dead and slain!

II
"Lo, thou hast broken the sweet yoke
   That my high beauty held above          10
All priests and clerks and merchant-folk;
   There was not one but for my love
   Would give me gold and gold enough,
Though sorrow his very heart had riven,
   To win from me such wage thereof
As now no thief would take if given.

III
"I was right chary of the same,
   God wot it was my great folly,
For love of one sly knave of them,
   Good store of that same sweet had he;        20
   For all my subtle wiles, perdie,
God wot I loved him well enow;
   Right evilly he handled me,
But he loved well my gold, I trow.

IV
"Though I gat bruises green and black,
   I loved him never the less a jot;
Though he bound burdens on my back,
   If he said 'Kiss me and heed it not'
   Right little pain I felt, God wot,

When that foul thief's mouth, found so sweet,
    Kissed me—Much good thereof I got!
I keep the sin and the shame of it.

V
"And he died thirty year agone.
    I am old now, no sweet thing to see;
By God, though, when I think thereon,
    And of that good glad time, woe's me,
    And stare upon my changed body
Stark naked, that has been so sweet,
    Lean, wizen, like a small dry tree,
I am nigh mad with the pain of it.

VI
"Where is my faultless forehead's white,
    The lifted eyebrows, soft gold hair,
Eyes wide apart and keen of sight,
    With subtle skill in the amorous air;
    The straight nose, great nor small, but fair,
The small carved ears of shapeliest growth,
    Chin dimpling, colour good to wear,
And sweet red splendid kissing mouth?

VII
"The shapely slender shoulders small,
    Long arms, hands wrought in glorious wise,
Round little breasts, the hips withal
    High, full of flesh, not scant of size,
    Fit for all amorous masteries;
The large loins, and the flower that was
    Planted above my strong round thighs
In a small garden of soft grass?

VIII
"A writhled forehead, hair gone grey,
    Fallen eyebrows, eyes gone blind and red,
Their laughs and looks all fled away,
    Yea, all that smote men's hearts are fled;

The bowed nose, fallen from goodlihead;
Foul flapping ears like water-flags;
   Peaked chin, and cheeks all waste and dead,
And lips that are two skinny rags:

IX
"Thus endeth all the beauty of us.
   The arms made short, the hands made lean,
The shoulders bowed and ruinous,
   The breasts, alack! all fallen in;
   The flanks too, like the breasts, grown thin;
As for the sweet place, out on it!                                          70
   For the lank thighs, no thighs but skin,
They are specked with spots like sausage-meat.

X
"So we make moan for the old sweet days,
   Poor old light women, two or three
Squatting above the straw-fire's blaze,
   The bosom crushed against the knee,
   Like faggots on a heap we be,
Round fires soon lit, soon quenched and done;
   And we were once so sweet, even we!
Thus fareth many and many an one."                                  80

# from Tristram of Lyonesse

## *from* Canto I: The Sailing of the Swallow

    And her heart sprang in Iseult, and she drew
With all her spirit and life the sunrise through,
And through her lips the keen triumphant air
Sea-scented, sweeter than land-roses were,     440
And through her eyes the whole rejoicing east
Sun-satisfied, and all the heaven at feast
Spread for the morning; and the imperious mirth
Of wind and light that moved upon the earth,
Making the spring, and all the fruitful might
And strong regeneration of delight
That swells the seedling leaf and sapling man,
Since the first life in the first world began
To burn and burgeon through void limbs and veins,
And the first love with sharp sweet procreant pains     450
To pierce and bring forth roses; yea, she felt
Through her own soul the sovereign morning melt,
And all the sacred passion of the sun;
And as the young clouds flamed and were undone
About him coming, touched and burnt away
In rosy ruin and yellow spoil of day,
The sweet veil of her body and corporal sense
Felt the dawn also cleave it, and incense
With light from inward and with effluent heat
The kindling soul through fleshly hands and feet.     460
And as the august great blossom of the dawn
Burst, and the full sun scarce from sea withdrawn
Seemed on the fiery water a flower afloat,
So as a fire the mighty morning smote
Throughout her, and incensed with the influent hour
Her whole soul's one great mystical red flower
Burst, and the bud of her sweet spirit broke
Rose-fashion, and the strong spring at a stroke
Thrilled, and was cloven, and from the full sheath came
The whole rose of the woman red as flame:     470

And all her Mayday blood as from a swoon
Flushed, and May rose up in her and was June.
So for a space her heart as heavenward burned:
Then with half summer in her eyes she turned,
And on her lips was April yet, and smiled,
As though the spirit and sense unreconciled
Shrank laughing back, and would not ere its hour
Let life put forth the irrevocable flower.

* * *

   For Tristram being athirst with toil now spake,    751
Saying, "Iseult, for all dear love's labour's sake
Give me to drink, and give me for a pledge
The touch of four lips on the beaker's edge."
And Iseult sought and would not wake Brangwain
Who slept as one half dead with fear and pain,
Being tender-natured; so with hushed light feet
Went Iseult round her, with soft looks and sweet
Pitying her pain; so sweet a spirited thing
She was, and daughter of a kindly king.    760
And spying what strange bright secret charge was kept
Fast in that maid's white bosom while she slept,
She sought and drew the gold cup forth and smiled
Marvelling, with such light wonder as a child
That hears of glad sad life in magic lands;
And bare it back to Tristram with pure hands
Holding the love-draught that should be for flame
To burn out of them fear and faith and shame,
And lighten all their life up in men's sight,
And make them sad for ever. Then the knight    770
Bowed toward her and craved whence had she this strange thing
That might be spoil of some dim Asian king,
By starlight stolen from some waste place of sands,
And a maid bore it here in harmless hands.
And Iseult, laughing—"Other lords that be
Feast, and their men feast after them; but we,
Our men must keep the best wine back to feast
Till they be full and we of all men least

Feed after them and fain to fare so well:
So with mine handmaid and your squire it fell 780
That hid this bright thing from us in a wile:"
And with light lips yet full of their swift smile,
And hands that wist not though they dug a grave,
Undid the hasps of gold, and drank, and gave,
And he drank after, a deep glad kingly draught:
And all their life changed in them, for they quaffed
Death; if it be death so to drink, and fare
As men who change and are what these twain were.
And shuddering with eyes full of fear and fire
And heart-stung with a serpentine desire 790
He turned and saw the terror in her eyes
That yearned upon him shining in such wise
As a star midway in the midnight fixed.
   Their Galahault was the cup, and she that mixed;
Nor other hand there needed, nor sweet speech
To lure their lips together; each on each
Hung with strange eyes and hovered as a bird
Wounded, and each mouth trembled for a word;
Their heads neared, and their hands were drawn in one,
And they saw dark, though still the unsunken sun 800
Far through fine rain shot fire into the south;
And their four lips became one burning mouth.

## *from* Canto II: The Queen's Pleasaunce

   There was a bower beyond man's eye more fair
Than ever summer dews and sunniest air 280
Fed full with rest and radiance till the boughs
Had wrought a roof as for a holier house
Than aught save love might breathe in; fairer far
Than keeps the sweet light back of moon and star
From high kings' chambers: there might love and sleep
Divide for joy the darkling hours, and keep
With amorous alternation of sweet strife
The soft and secret ways of death and life
Made smooth for pleasure's feet to rest and run

Even from the moondawn to the kindling sun, 290
Made bright for passion's feet to run and rest
Between the midnight's and the morning's breast,
Where hardly though her happy head lie down
It may forget the hour that wove its crown;
Where hardly though her joyous limbs be laid
They may forget the mirth that midnight made.
And thither, ere sweet night had slain sweet day,
Iseult and Tristram took their wandering way,
And rested, and refreshed their hearts with cheer
In hunters' fashion of the woods; and here 300
More sweet it seemed, while this might be, to dwell
And take of all world's weariness farewell
Than reign of all world's lordship queen and king.
Nor here would time for three moons' changes bring
Sorrow nor thought of sorrow; but sweet earth
Fostered them like her babes of eldest birth,
Reared warm in pathless woods and cherished well.
And the sun sprang above the sea and fell,
And the stars rose and sank upon the sea;
And outlaw-like, in forest wise and free, 310
The rising and the setting of their lights
Found those twain dwelling all those days and nights.
And under change of sun and star and moon
Flourished and fell the chaplets woven of June,
And fair through fervours of the deepening sky
Panted and passed the hours that lit July,
And each day blessed them out of heaven above,
And each night crowned them with the crown of love.
Nor till the might of August overhead
Weighed on the world was yet one roseleaf shed 320
Of all their joy's warm coronal, nor aught
Touched them in passing ever with a thought
That ever this might end on any day
Or any night not love them where they lay;
But like a babbling tale of barren breath
Seemed all report and rumour held of death,
And a false bruit the legend tear-impearled
That such a thing as change was in the world.

And each bright song upon his lips that came,
Mocking the powers of change and death by name,     330
Blasphemed their bitter godhead, and defied
Time, though clothed round with ruin as kings with pride,
To blot the glad life out of love: and she
Drank lightly deep of his philosophy
In that warm wine of amorous words which is
Sweet with all truths of all philosophies.
For well he wist all subtle ways of song,
And in his soul the secret eye was strong
That burns in meditation, till bright words
Break flamelike forth as notes from fledgeling birds     340
That feel the soul speak through them of the spring.
So fared they night and day as queen and king
Crowned of a kingdom wide as day and night.
Nor ever cloudlet swept or swam in sight
Across the darkling depths of their delight
Whose stars no skill might number, nor man's art
Sound the deep stories of its heavenly heart.
Till, even for wonder that such life should live,
Desires and dreams of what death's self might give
Would touch with tears and laughter and wild speech     350
The lips and eyes of passion, fain to reach,
Beyond all bourne of time or trembling sense,
The verge of love's last possible eminence.
Out of the heaven that storm nor shadow mars,
Deep from the starry depth beyond the stars,
A yearning ardour without scope or name
Fell on them, and the bright night's breath of flame
Shot fire into their kisses; and like fire
The lit dews lightened on the leaves, as higher
Night's heart beat on toward midnight. Far and fain     360
Somewhiles the soft rush of rejoicing rain
Solaced the darkness, and from steep to steep
Of heaven they saw the sweet sheet lightning leap
And laugh its heart out in a thousand smiles,
When the clear sea for miles on glimmering miles
Burned as though dawn were strewn abroad astray,
Or, showering out of heaven, all heaven's array

Had paven instead the waters: fain and far
Somewhiles the burning love of star for star
Spake words that love might wellnigh seem to hear     370
In such deep hours as turn delight to fear
Sweet as delight's self ever. So they lay
Tranced once, nor watched along the fiery bay
The shine of summer darkness palpitate and play.
She had nor sight nor voice; her swooning eyes
Knew not if night or light were in the skies;
Across her beauty sheer the moondawn shed
Its light as on a thing as white and dead;
Only with stress of soft fierce hands she prest
Between the throbbing blossoms of her breast          380
His ardent face, and through his hair her breath
Went quivering as when life is hard on death;
And with strong trembling fingers she strained fast
His head into her bosom; till at last,
Satiate with sweetness of that burning bed,
His eyes afire with tears, he raised his head
And laughed into her lips; and all his heart
Filled hers; then face from face fell, and apart
Each hung on each with panting lips, and felt
Sense into sense and spirit in spirit melt.            390
  "Hast thou no sword? I would not live till day;
O love, this night and we must pass away,
It must die soon, and let not us die late."
  "Take then my sword and slay me; nay, but wait
Till day be risen; what, wouldst thou think to die
Before the light take hold upon the sky?"
  "Yea, love; for how shall we have twice, being twain,
This very night of love's most rapturous reign?
Live thou and have thy day, and year by year
Be great, but what shall I be? Slay me here;           400
Let me die not when love lies dead, but now
Strike through my heart: nay, sweet, what heart hast thou?
Is it so much I ask thee, and spend my breath
In asking? nay, thou knowest it is but death.
Hadst thou true heart to love me, thou wouldst give
This: but for hate's sake thou wilt let me live."

    Here he caught up her lips with his, and made
The wild prayer silent in her heart that prayed,
And strained her to him till all her faint breath sank
And her bright light limbs palpitated and shrank410
And rose and fluctuated as flowers in rain
That bends them and they tremble and rise again
And heave and straighten and quiver all through with bliss
And turn afresh their mouths up for a kiss,
Amorous, athirst of that sweet influent love;
So, hungering towards his hovering lips above,
Her red-rose mouth yearned silent, and her eyes
Closed, and flashed after, as through June's darkest skies
The divine heartbeats of the deep live light
Make open and shut the gates of the outer night.420

# Explanatory Notes

[These notes, far from comprehensive, aim to specify the first book publication of each poem or passage, translate foreign phrases, identify unfamiliar proper names, and provide minimal context for excerpted passages.]

### from *Chastelard: A Tragedy* (1865)
At the opening of the last act of Swinburne's play, the French poet Chastelard, passionately in love with Mary, Queen of Scots, awaits execution for having concealed himself in the Queen's bedchamber.

42: *Paphian*: Paphos on Cypus was a centre of the cult of Aphrodite.

### A Ballad of Life (*Poems and Ballads*, 1866)
76: *Borgia*: the Renaissance *femme fatale* Lucrezia Borgia (1480-1519), notorious for her sexual adventurousness and cruelty.

### Laus Veneris (*Poems and Ballads*, 1866)
Title: 'Praise of Venus' (Latin). Swinburne's version of the Tannhäuser myth is narrated in the voice of that thirteenth-century German knight-minstrel, who sojourned with Venus in her mountain (the Horsel); after repenting his sin but being denied absolution by the pope, Tannhäuser returned to the arms of the goddess. The opening epigraph, in Swinburne's imitation Renaissance French, can be translated as follows:

> Then he said, weeping; Alas, too unfortunate man and cursed sinner, I will never see the mercy and pity of God. Now I will go from here and hide myself within Mount Horsel, begging the favour and the the loving mercy of my sweet lady Venus, for whose love I will be damned forever to hell. This is the end of all my feats of arms and all my beautiful songs. Alas, too beautiful were the face of my lady and her eyes, and it was an evil day that I saw them. Then he went away groaning and returned to her, and lived there sadly in great love with his lady. It happened afterwards that one day the pope saw beautiful red and white flowers and many leafy buds break forth on his staff, and he saw all the bark become green again. Then he was much afraid and moved, and a great pity seized him for the knight who had left without hope, like a man miserable and damned. So he sent many messengers to bring him back, saying that he would have grace and good absolution from God for his great sin of love. But they saw him no more; for the poor knight dwelled forever with Venus, the high and mighty goddess, in the flanks of the mountain of love. *Book of the great marvels of love, written in Latin and French by Master Antoine Gaget.* 1530.

133: *Adonis*: mortal lover of Aphrodite/Venus, slain by a wild boar.
200: *Semiramis*: semi-legendary Assyrian queen, singled out by Dante and others for her lustfulness.
425: EXPLICIT LAUS VENERIS: (Latin) 'Here ends the praise of Venus'.

### Les Noyades (*Poems and Ballads*, 1866)
Title: 'The Drownings' (French); during the Reign of Terror in the French Revolution, some 4,000 people accused of counter-revolutionary activities were summarily executed by drowning in Nantes.

9: *Carrier*: Jean-Baptiste Carrier (1756-1794) was sent to Nantes in 1793 by the National Convention to suppress the counter-revolution.

### Anactoria (*Poems and Ballads*, 1866)
The poem is in the voice of the seventh century BCE Sappho of Lesbos, whom Swinburne considered the greatest poet who ever lived. Her work survives almost entirely in fragments. *Anactoria*, mentioned in fragment 16, is a former lover of Sappho's. The epigraph emends a passage from Sappho's only complete poem, the famous 'Hymn to Aphrodite': 'Whose love have you vainly caught by persuasion?'

22: *Erotion or Erinna*: the female name Erinna occurs in several of Sappho's fragments; 'Erotion', presumably a male name, is a diminutive of 'Eros.'
64: *Paphos*: see note to l. 42 of *Chastelard*.
73-4: *"Who doth thee wrong, / Sappho?"*: a translation of Sappho's lines directly following the epigraph.
81-4: *"Even she...wouldst not"*: a translation of the sixth stanza of the Aphrodite hymn.
169: *Pleiads*: the constellation of the Pleiades was identified with the seven daughters of Atlas and Pleione; Sappho mentions them in the famous fragment 168B.
195: *Pierian flower*: Pieria was the homeland of the Muses, thus Pierian roses were symbolic of the Muses' productions; see Sappho, fragment 55.
286: *Atthis*: a former lover of Sappho's, named in a number of fragments (8, 96, 131).
302: *Lotus and Lethe*: the lotus flower induces drowsiness, the waters of the underworld river Lethe forgetfulness.

### Hermaphroditus (*Poems and Ballads*, 1866)
As the dateline at the end of the poem indicates, Swinburne saw the classical sculpture known as the 'Sleeping Hermaphrodite' in the Louvre in 1863.

53: *Salmacis*: In Ovid's *Metamorphoses* IV, the water nymph Salmacis loves the youth Hermaphroditus; she seizes him, and the two merge into a single body.

**Fragoletta** (*Poems and Ballads*, 1866)
Title: 'Little Strawberry' (Italian), probably alluding to the novel *Fragoletta ou Naples et Paris en 1799* (1829) by Henri de Latouche (1785-1851), which tells the story of a hermaphrodite of that name.

**Satia Te Sanguine** (*Poems and Ballads*, 1866)
Title: 'Glut Yourself with Blood' (Latin). According to Herodotus, the Scythian queen Tomyris (or 'Thomyris', as in 'The Masque of Queen Bersabe' below) defeated the Persian emperor Cyrus the Great, had him beheaded, and thrust his head into a wineskin filled with blood, saying (in the Latin of various medieval sources) 'satia te sanguine quem sitisti' (glut yourself with the blood for which you have thirsted).

**In the Orchard** (*Poems and Ballads*, 1866)
This poem, as its subtitle indicates, is an exercise in the Provençal *alba*, a 'dawn-song' in which the lover laments his imminent separation from the beloved. A 'burden' is a refrain, as in the repeated line at the end of each stanza.

**A Match** (*Poems and Ballads*, 1866)

**Faustine** (*Poems and Ballads*, 1866)
Two women, both named Annia Galeria Faustina, were associated with the Roman emperor Marcus Aurelius (AD 121-180): one his aunt, the other (daughter to the first) his wife. Both were renowned for licentiousness and deception. The epigraph, which means 'Hail, Empress Faustina, we who are about to die salute you', echoes what is popularly remembered as Roman gladiators' greeting to the Emperor.

99: *Bacchanal*: a worshipper of Bacchus, god of wine (l. 101).
118: *Mitylene*: the town on the island of Lesbos from which Sappho hailed.
146: *Lampascene*: Lampascus was the seat of the cult of the phallic god Priapus.

**A Cameo** (*Poems and Ballads*, 1866)

**The Leper** (*Poems and Ballads*, 1866)
The final prose note, in Swinburne's imitation Renaissance French, can be translated as follows:

> At that time there were a great number of lepers in the land, which greatly displeased the king, seeing that because of them the Lord must have been grievously angered. It happened that a noble lady named Yolande de

Sallières was afflicted and entirely ravaged by this base illness, and all her friends and her parents (having the fear of God before their eyes) made her leave their houses, and would neither receive nor aid a thing cursed of God and stinking and abominable to all men. That lady had been very beautiful and graceful of form, of a generous figure and lascivious lifestyle. However none of the lovers who had frequently embraced and kissed her so tenderly would harbour any longer such a ugly woman and such a detestable sinner. But one clerk, who had been first her servant and her go-between in matters of love, took her in and hid her in a small hut. There she died of great misery an evil death: and afterwards the clerk died, who out of his great love for her had for six months tended, washed, dressed and undressed her every day with his own hands. It is even said that this evil man and cursed clerk, remembering this woman's great beauty (now passed and ravaged), delighted many times to kissed her on her unclean and leprous mouth and to embrace her sweetly with loving hands. Therefore he died of that same abominable illness. This took place near Fontainebellant in Gastinois. And when King Philip heard the story, he was very astonished. *Grand Chronicles of France*, 1505.

**Erotion** (*Poems and Ballads*, 1866)
Title: see note to line 21 of 'Anactoria'.

**Before Dawn** (*Poems and Ballads*, 1866)

**Dolores** (*Poems and Ballads*, 1866)
The name 'Dolores' derives from the epithet for the Virgin Mary, 'Our Lady of Seven Sorrows', which Swinburne cites in French as his subtitle.

51: *Libitina, Priapus*: Libitina is a Roman (not quite 'Tuscan') goddess historically misidentified with Venus; Priapus is the god of gardens, notorious for his erect phallus.
223: *Thalassian*: having to do with the sea: an epithet of Venus, who rose from the waves.
299: *Alciphron, Arisbe*: though these names occur in Greek mythology, Swinburne seems to have no particular allusion in mind.
307: The passage in the footnote (now thought not to be by Catullus) can be translated 'For you [Priapus] especially the coast of the Hellespont—more abundant in oysters than the rest—worships in its cities."
326: *Ipsithilla*: a woman addressed in Catullus' Carmina 32.
330: *the Phrygian*: the self-castrated Phrygian priests of the Mother Goddess Cybele.

333: *Ida*: The Romans identified Cybele as the 'Idaean mother', after Mount Ida in Phrygia.

340: *Catullus*: the Roman poet Gaius Valerius Catullus (c. 84–c. 54 BCE), known in part for his erotic poems, and alluded to or quoted elsewhere in the poem (l. 307, l. 326).

345: *Dindymus*: Mount Didymus in Phrygia, centre and origin of the cult of Cybele.

405: *Lampsacus*: the centre of the cult of Priapus (see l. 51).

406: *Aphaca*: in Lebanon, the birthplace of Adonis (see 'Laus Veneris', note to l. 133) and site of the temple of Aphrodite Aphakitis.

409-10: *Cotytto, Astarte, Ashtaroth*: Cotytto is a Thracian goddess; Astarte and Ashtaroth are Ishtar, the Mesopotamian goddess of love.

### Sapphics (*Poems and Ballads*, 1866)

'Sapphics' is the name given to the stanza and metre in which Sappho wrote.

16: Mitylene: see 'Faustine', note to l. 117.
76: Lethe: The river of the underworld whose waters imparted forgetfulness.

### *from* The Masque of Queen Bersabe: A Miracle-Play (*Poems and Ballads*, 1866)

'The Masque of Queen Bersabe' is Swinburne's imitation of a medieval miracle play, complete with Latin stage directions. It is a version of the story of King David and his adulterous affair with Bathsheba (2 Samuel 11-12). Where the biblical Bathsheba is a passive figure, Swinburne's Bersabe is a *femme fatale*, and his play culminates in the prophet Nathan's presenting the queen with a procession of twenty-two infamous women from antiquity. Some of them are historical, biblical, or mythological figures with relevant back-stories, but others' names seem to have been taken largely at random from scripture or the classical legendarium; only the former have been annotated here.

*Herodias*: according to the Gospels of Matthew and Mark, Herodias (c. 15-after 39 CE), wife of the Tetrarch Herod Antipas, procured the execution of John the Baptist through her daughter Salome's dancing; Swinburne implies here that Herodias herself danced.

*Aholibah*: in Ezekiel 23, an allegorical figure lusting after the Assyrians.

*Cleopatra*: see headnote to 'Cleopatra' below.

*Aholah*: in Ezekiel 23, the sister of Aholibah.

*Semiramis*: see note to l. 200 of 'Laus Veneris'.

*Hesione*: daughter of Laomedon, King of Troy, and saved by Heracles from a sea monster.

*Chrysothemis*: daughter of Agamemnon.

*Thomyris*: see headnote to 'Satia te Sanguine'.

*Myrrha*: in Ovid's *Metamorphoses*, the daughter and lover of Cinyras of Panchaia.

*Pasiphae*: see headnote to 'Pasiphae' below.

*Sappho*: see headnote to 'Anactoria'.

*Messalina*: third wife of the Emperor Claudius, Messalina (17/20-48 CE) was notorious for promiscuity.

*Amestris*: wife of Xerxes I of Persia, whose cruelty towards her rival in beauty is recorded in Herodotus.

*Alaciel*: in Boccaccio's *Decameron*, the daughter of the Sultan of Babylon and wife of the King Algarve; after sleeping with nine men, she was still taken for a virgin.

*Erigone*: daughter of Icarius, taught by Dionysus how to make wine.

**Love and Sleep** (*Poems and Ballads*, 1866)

**Cleopatra** (*The Cornhill*, September 1866; uncollected in Swinburne's lifetime)

Cleopatra (69-30 BCE) was the last Ptolemaic ruler of Egypt, lover of Julius Caesar and Marc Antony. She was widely celebrated for her beauty, political craft, and powers of seduction, and was notably depicted by Chaucer, Boccaccio, and Shakespeare. The epigraph is Swinburne's invention.

88: Actium: At the naval battle of Actium (31 BCE), Marc Antony's fleet was defeated by Octavian after the ships commanded by Antony's lover Cleopatra unexpectedly withdrew.

*from* **Pasiphae [a dramatic fragment]** (unpublished)

Swinburne began this imitation Greek tragedy—presumably something of a companion piece to the dramatic vignette 'Phædra' in *Poems and Ballads*—in 1867, but never took it beyond rough draft stage. The text here follows Catherine Maxwell's transcription of the manuscript, with speech prefixes expanded but ampersands and a few metrical solecisms unaltered. The bulk of the fragment is reprinted here, omitting only the last few (largely unrelated) lines, spoken by Pasiphae's nurse.

Pasiphaë was the wife of the Cretan king Minos. Seized with desire for a white bull sent by Poseidon, she sought the help of the inventor-artificer Daedalus, who fashioned a lifelike artificial cow within which Pasiphaë could crouch and mate with the animal. (The offspring of this coupling would be the half-human, half-bovine Minotaur.) Pasiphaë's daughter Phædra, in Swinburne's 'Phædra', alludes to this episode: desire, she says,

> hath sown pain and plague in all our house,
> Love loathed of love, and mates unmatchable,
> Wild wedlock, and the lusts that bleat or low,
> And marriage-fodder snuffed about of kine.

**The Complaint of the Fair Armouress**
(*Poems and Ballads, Second Series*, 1873)
A translation of 'Les regrets de la belle heaulmière' by the French poet François Villon (1431-1463).

**from *Tristram of Lyonesse*** (*Tristram of Lyonesse and Other Poems*, 1882)
Swinburne's long Arthurian poem, begun in 1869 but not published in full until 1882, is of a piece with the medievalist enthusiasms of his Pre-Raphaelite friends Rossetti and Morris. Swinburne despised the Victorian pieties of Tennyson's *Idylls of the King*, which he called the 'Morte d'Albert'. In his own version of the Tristan and Isolde story, he wrote Rossetti in 1870, 'I hope to make copulative passages... more warm and provocative of sinful appetite than anything my chaste Muse has yet attempted'.

*from* Canto I: The Sailing of the Swallow
The knight Tristram has been sent by King Mark of Cornwall to escort to him his betrothed, princess Iseult of Ireland. Unbeknownst to the two, the queen has entrusted Iseult's handmaiden Brangwain with a magic love-potion to seal her marriage to Mark. On the passage from Ireland to Cornwall, Tristram and Iseult through mischance drink the love-potion, which confirms them in the mutual passion that has already begun to spring up between them.

794: *Galahaunt*: in some Arthurian sources, Galahaunt (or Galehaut) is the knight who faciliates the liaison of Lancelot and Guineve; in Dante's *Inferno* V, his book is the one Paolo and Francesca are reading when they succumb to their illicit love.

*from* Canto II: The Queen's Pleasaunce
Iseult and Mark are married, but Iseult deceives the king by substituting Brangwain for herself in his bed so that the marriage is not consummated. In his cups King Mark rashly offers the knight-minstrel Palamede anything he desires; Palamede claims Iseult and carries her away. Tristram rescues Iseult, and bears her off to an idyllic bower where they consummate their love.

www.ingramcontent.com/pod-product-compliance
Lightning Source LLC
Chambersburg PA
CBHW031154160426
43193CB00008B/366